HELPING YOURSELF WITH WHITE MAGIC

ROBERT PELTON

ORIGINAL PUBLICATIONS

PLAINVIEW, NEW YORK

Special thanks to Maria Solomon the author of
"Helping Yourself with Magical Oils A-Z"
for her editorial assistance on this project.

COPYRIGHT © 1998 ORIGINAL PUBLICATIONS

ISBN: 0-942272-52-6

All Rights Reserved.
No portion of this book may be reproduced in any form
or by any means without written permission from the Publisher.

ORIGINAL PUBLICATIONS
P.O. BOX 236
OLD BETHPAGE, NEW YORK 11804-0236
1 (888) OCCULT-1

VISIT US ON THE WEB AT:
WWW.ORIGINALPUBLICATIONS.COM

The Author and Publisher offer the content of this book for interest, folklore value, experimentation and whatever value it may have to the reader thereof. Please be advised that we cannot make any claims of supernatural effects or powers for any of the formulas, spells, rituals, etc. listed herein. This book is offered as literary curio only. No responsibility whatsoever for the contents or veracity of the statements herein is assumed by the author, publisher or seller of this book.

TABLE OF CONTENTS

PREFACE

1. **White Magic Candle Burning** 1
   - *Monthly Vibratory Candle Chart* 2
   - *Daily Cross Candle Chart* 2
   - *Procedure for Properly Lighting Candles* 3

2. **Standard Altar Arrangements** 4
   - *Private Sessions (Alone)* 4
   - *Consultation Sessions (with One Other Person)* 5
   - *Small Group Meetings (7 People or Less)* 6
   - *Large Group Meetings (Over 7 People)* 7

3. **Seating Arrangements and Ritual Procedures** 8
   - *Private Session (Alone)* 9
   - *Consultation Sessions (with One Other Person)* 10
   - *Small Group Meetings (7 People or Less)* 10
   - *Large Group Meetings (Over 7 People)* 11
   - *Conducting a Proper Novena* 12
   - *To Gain Spiritual Assistance* 13
   - *To Become a Spiritualist or Medium* 14
   - *To Gain Spiritual Strength* 14

4. **Invocations for Love and Marriage** 16
   - *When Your Wife Walks Out on You* 16
   - *To Regain a Lover* 17
   - *To Become More Sexually Exciting* 18
   - *To Gain Peace in the Home* 18
   - *To Help Find a New Sweetheart* 19
   - *When Your Husband Leaves* 20
   - *To Regain Happiness in Love* 21
   - *When You Lose a Sweetheart* 22

5. **Invocations to Draw Good Fortune** 23
   - *To Obtain General Success* 23
   - *To Quickly Gain New Friendships* 23
   - *To Develop Happiness* 24
   - *To Powerfully Influence Others* 25
   - *To Accomplish Your Goals* 26
   - *How to Get a Good Job* 27
   - *To Hold a Job Under All Circumstances* 27
   - *To Change Your Luck* 29

6. **Invocations to Gain Financially** 31
   - *When Good Luck Evades You* 31
   - *To Increase Your Finances* 31

To Become More Prosperous 32
To Draw More Business 33
To Gain Gambling Luck 34
To Improve Your Business 35
To Improve Your General Conditions 37

7. Invocations for Overcoming Evil. 38
To Stop Gossip and Slander 38
To Overcome Suffering 39
To Rid Yourself of Evil Thoughts 40
To Stop Legal Persecution 41
To Control Troublemakers 42
To Protect Against Imprisonment 43
To Remove Evil Influences 44

8. Secret Spells for Drawing Love 46
To Increase the Passion of a Lover 46
To Sexually Control Someone With Sensuality 47
To Incite a Desired Lover to Passion 47
To Gain More Than One Good Lover 48
To Protect Against Being Hurt by a False Lover 48
To Improve the Quality of Lovemaking 49
To Stop a Lover From Becoming Jealous or Possessive 50
To Totally Gain Control Over a Lover 51
A Special Spell for Attracting New Love 51

9. Secret Spells for a Happy Marriage 53
To Force a Lover to Marry You 53
To Aid in Your Marriage Prospects 54
To Bring More Lovemaking to Your Marriage Bed 54
To Force Your Partner to Stay Faithful 55
To Find the Perfect Marriage Mate 55
To Force a Wandering Mate to Return 56
To Dream Who Your Future Mate Will Be 57
To Bring Forth a Proposal of Marriage 58
To Discover a Suitable Mate Among Your Friends 58
To Stop a Wayward Mate From Seeing a Lover 59

10. Secret Spells for Drawing Good Fortune 60
To Overcome Adversity 60
To Attract Luckier Vibrations in Your Life 61
To Overwhelm All Bad Luck 61
To Make Better Things Happen in Your Life 62
To Attract Much Better Luck and Fortune 63
To Help Bring Good Fortune to Your Life 63
To Improve Your Life's Position and Status 64

11. Secret Spells for Financial Gain 65
    To Attract Lots of Money 65
    To Better Succeed and Make Money 66
    To Obtain a Raise on the Job 66
    To Bring More Money and Success in Everything 67
    To Overcome Financial Reverses 67
    To Receive a Financial Blessing When in Need 68
    To Make Your Financial Prospects Much Better 69

12. Secret Spells for Protection From Harm 70
    To Avoid any Legal Trouble 70
    To Influence Someone Who Hates You 71
    To Remove All Obstacles from Your Path 71
    To Change an Enemy's Mind 72
    To Stop a Thief Before He Steals From You 72
    To Restrain Someone Who is Causing Distress 73
    To Drive Insanity Away From You & Into Someone Else 75
    A Powerful Spell to Overcome All Problems 75
    To Overcome Disfavor 76
    To Compel a Thief to Return Stolen Goods 77

13. Secret Spells Against Illness and Death 79
    To Overcome Any Kind of Illness 79
    Special Spell to Help Avoid Accidents 80
    To Escape All Forms of Serious Sickness 80
    To Make a Sick Person Feel Much Better 81
    To Stop Mental Illness 82
    To Prevent Any Physical Harm 83
    Special Spell to Protect Against Untimely Death 83
    To Relieve Pain During Illness 84

14. Secret Spells for the Destruction of Evil 85
    To Force an Enemy to Stop Harming You 85
    To Break the Influence of an Evil Spell 86
    To Eliminate Danger From Your Life 86
    To Stop the Effects of an Evil Eye Spell 87
    To Force a Malicious Person to Leave You Alone 87
    A Powerful Evil Destroying Charm 88
    To Reverse A Bad Spell's Disastrous Effect 89
    To Make Someone Stop Hexing You 90
    To Defeat A Dangerous Rival 90
    To Bind a Person Who is Exerting Evil Power 91

Preface

The history of white magic goes far back into antiquity. It began with the first man in the darkness of a cave. He no doubt lit a crudely constructed candle of sorts, or babbled a few select utterances to his gods in order to induce rain during the dry months, to bring about the sunrise, increase his luck in a hunt for food, or for innumerable other things. As Arthur Edward Waite writes in **The Book of Black Magic:** *"The desire to communicate with the spirits is older than history; it connects with ineradicable principles in human nature."*

White magic rituals and practices have been handed down since time immemorial—by word of mouth, manuscripts, and highly specialized books. Waite again states: *"Between the most ancient processes, such as those of Chaldean Magic, and the rites of the Middle Ages, there are marked correspondences."*

Man, ever superstitious, has always utilized occult powers for the betterment of himself. White magic has flourished more widely in our century than at any time since the 1500's. We have witnessed a continuing rise in all areas of occult study, and the direct application of such knowledge by man. The twentieth century has indeed been a period of general enlightenment.

Although the present age is often characterized as one of materialism and of late dominated by computers, the supernatural continues, ironically, to play a more vital part in all our lives. The vast majority of people, young and old, are superstitious to some degree. A number of people today believe in witchcraft, astrology, numerology, and other supernatural sciences. Others are deeply religious. The supernatural envelops all of us; it reaches us in our churches, our dreams, our drug culture, our newspapers, our television shows.

In **Dogme et Rituel de la Haute Magie,** *1854,* Eliphas Levi gives this advice: *"Let us start by declaring that we believe in all miracles, because we are convinced and certain, even by our own experience, of their complete possibility. There are some which we do not attempt to explain, but which we consider to be none the less explicable."*

PREFACE

C. G. Jung, the renowned psychologist, was deeply interested in astrology and many other forms of the occult including the "I Ching." He used astrology in conjunction with his medical training for the diagnosis of his patients. Dr. Jung wrote: *"I can point to the easily verifiable fact that the heyday of astrology was not in the benighted Middle Ages but is in the middle of the twentieth century, when even the newspapers do not hesitate to publish the week's horoscope."*

White magic is completely opposed to the aims of black magic, or what is more commonly known as the "black arts." White magic is a magical practice which man uses only for good works; the warding-off of evil of all kinds, overcoming temptations, increasing personal power, gaining wealth, and improving the general conditions of one's life. As Franz Hartmann writes in **Magic White and Black;** *"The art of magic is the art of employing invisible or so-called spiritual agencies to obtain certain visible results."*

White magic may be defined as man's manipulation of natural universal forces, forces which are seldom fully understood and even less often admitted to exist. In *The Book of Black Magic*, Waite states it this way: "White ceremonial magic is an attempt to communicate with Good Spirits for a good, or at least an innocent purpose. Black magic is the attempt to communicate with Evil Spirits for an evil purpose.

Not so very long ago, telepathy (ESP) was believed to be a supernatural experience. ESP was doubted and ridiculed by most people. Hypnotism was classed in the occult realm. Thunder and lighning, and night and day, were said to be supernatural occurences. Today we show clear evidence these powers are not supernatural in the least. Each is now recognized and better understood in varying degrees. Hartman further clarifies magic when he writes: *"Magic may be said to be that science which deals with the mental moral powers of man, and shows what control he may exercise over himself and others."*

White magic is a serious practice. It is a tremendously exciting art. **Helping Yourself with White Magic** is unique to say the very least. It is most certainly a revelation - a practical guide to the proper utilization of this long secret mystical art. It is all embracing and contains information on all aspects of this occult science. Everything is thoroughly covered - from candle burning and reciting Psalms, and incense use to sprinkling powders and pouring oils. White magic is not difficult to understand or put into practice. No special talent or occult powers are required.

Helping Yourself with White Magic offers standardized services, rituals, and rites which are practiced throughout the world today. It is complete and can be readily adapted for use in large and small groups, or by an individual. All of the necessary information is given in a concise and easily understood format.

Any reader can follow the directions given herein and successfully master the age-old art of white magic. The simplicity of certain techniques and rites may surprise you. The tools are for your and for your friends' self-betterment. Use these fascinating tools wisely and with discretion.

1

WHITE MAGIC CANDLE BURNING

Prayer meetings, white magic circles, classes, or any other occult gathering must always burn seven colored candles. These seven special candles are commonly called white magic *Spectrum Candles* and consist of one blue, one orange, one pink, one purple, one red, one white, and one yellow.

Small worship groups of seven persons or less are required to burn only two white *Spiritual Candles* in lieu of the above seven Spectrum Candles.

The person who conducts either a large or small white magic service must also burn two special candles which are believed to be harmonious with his or her personal vibrations. Such candles are also to be burned in private sessions and while in consultation with anyone seeking assistance. While in consultation, your personal vibratory candles as well as those of the other party are to be burned, or four vibratory candles in all.

The proper selection of vibratory candles is determined by the month in which your birth took place. *Monthly Vibratory Candles,* as this type is called, are classified by color in two specific groups Primary and Secondary. Both Monthly Vibratory Candles must always be burned in unison. They are listed in the following table:

MONTHLY VIBRATORY CANDLE CHART

Birth Month	Primary	Secondary
January	Garnet	Silver-Gray
February	Dark Blue	Pink
March	Pink	White
April	White	Orange
May	Dark Blue	Gold
June	Light Blue	Red
July	Dark Green	Russet Brown
August	Light Green	Pink
September	Gold	Black
October	Red	Gold
November	Brown	Gold
December	Dark Green	Orange

For additional drawing power, special cross-shaped candles are to be burned at each private or group session. These are commonly called *Daily Cross Candles*. There are fourteen different colored candles in this group, two for each day of the week. The particular day on which white magic sessions are held determines which candle colors should be properly used. Daily Cross Candles are also classified in two distinct categories - *Primary and Secondary*. Both Daily Cross Candles must always be burned in unison. They are as listed in the following table:

DAILY CROSS CANDLE CHART

Day of Service	Primary	Secondary
Sunday	White	Gold
Monday	Pink	White
Tuesday	Bright Red	Pink
Wednesday	Dark Purple	Light violet
Thursday	Dark Blue	Light blue
Friday	Dark Green	Light green
Saturday	Black	Silver gray

White Magic Candle Burning

One or more *Special Purpose Candles,* classed by their respective colors, and determined by the specific purpose intended, are usually burned during white magic ceremonies. Each candle in this category is called for as required in the subsequent chapters.

Proper Candle Lighting Procedure

Candles have been placed in this world to provide the faithful person a means of showing their devotion in a tangible manner. You have the power to create whatsoever you will pertaining to human life. You have the power to determine what you shall create and when and where you wish to create it. Also you have the power to create what you want now.

It is recommended to those lighting candles that while doing so they make use of this prayer:

> *"May this offering I pray Thee, O Lord, both loose the bonds of my sins, and win for me the gift of thy blessed mercy."*

NOTE: Candles are and have been for centuries, used in the administration of every spiritual sacrament. Therefore, it is indispensable that every spiritual service, spiritual meditation, and any devotion spiritually connected should be conducted by candle light.

2

Standard Altar Arrangements

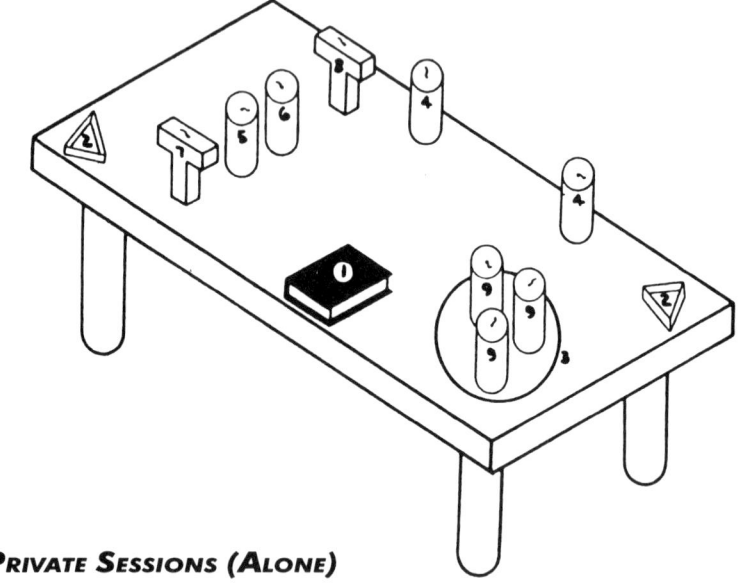

PRIVATE SESSIONS (ALONE)

The proper position of each item on the table or altar is as shown in the accompanying illustration. The numbers signify:

1. Bible
2. Triangular incense burners (can be any shape)
3. White chalk circle
4. Two White Spiritual Candles
5. Primary Monthly Vibratory Candle
6. Secondary Monthly Vibratory Candle
7. Primary Daily Cross Candle
8. Secondary Daily Cross Candle
9. Special Purpose Candles of varying colors. May be three or more (as called for in subsequent chapters).

Standard Altar Arrangements

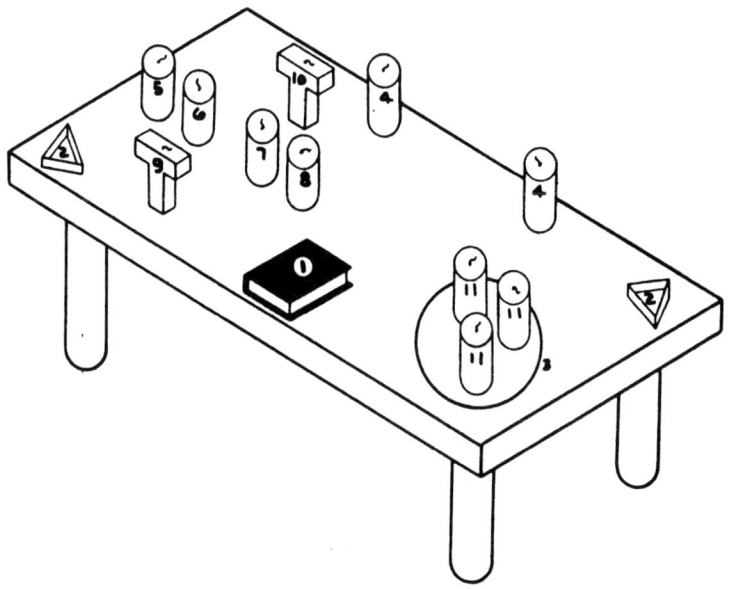

Consultation Sessions (with One Other Person)

The proper position of each item on the table or altar is as shown in the accompanying illustration. The numbers signify:

1. Bible
2. Triangular incense burners (can be any shape)
3. White chalk circle.
4. Two white Spiritual Candles
5. Primary Monthly Vibratory Candle
6. Primary Monthly Vibratory Candle
7. Secondary Monthly Vibratory Candle.
8. Secondary Monthly Vibratory Candle
9. Primary Daily Cross Candle
10. Secondary Daily Cross Candle
11. Special Purpose Candles of varying colors. May be three or more (as called for in subsequent chapters).

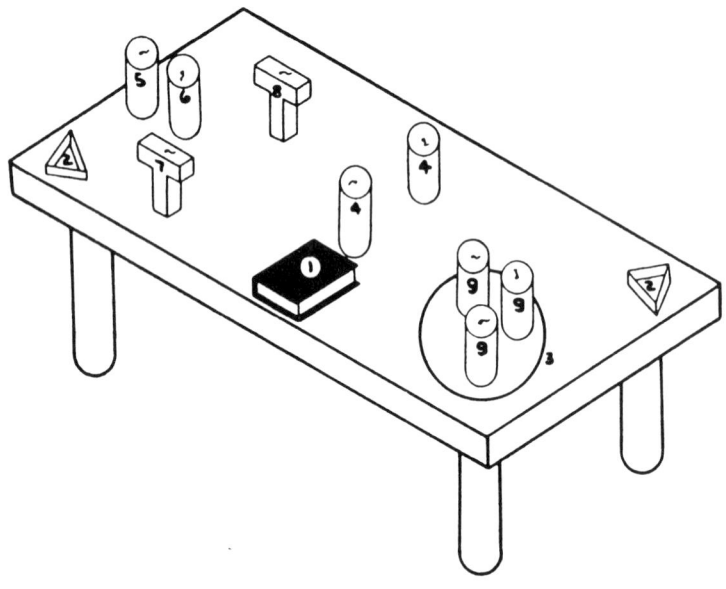

SMALL GROUP MEETINGS (SEVEN PEOPLE OR LESS)

The proper position of each item on the table or altar is as shown in the accompanying illustration. The numbers signify:

1. Bible
2. Triangular incense burners (can be any shape)
3. White chalk circle
4. Two white Spiritual Candles
5. Primary Monthly Vibratory Candle
6. Secondary Monthly Vibratory Candle.
7. Primary Daily Cross Candle
8. Secondary Daily Cross Candle
9. Special Purpose Candles of varying colors. May be three or more (as called for in subsequent chapters).

Standard Altar Arrangements

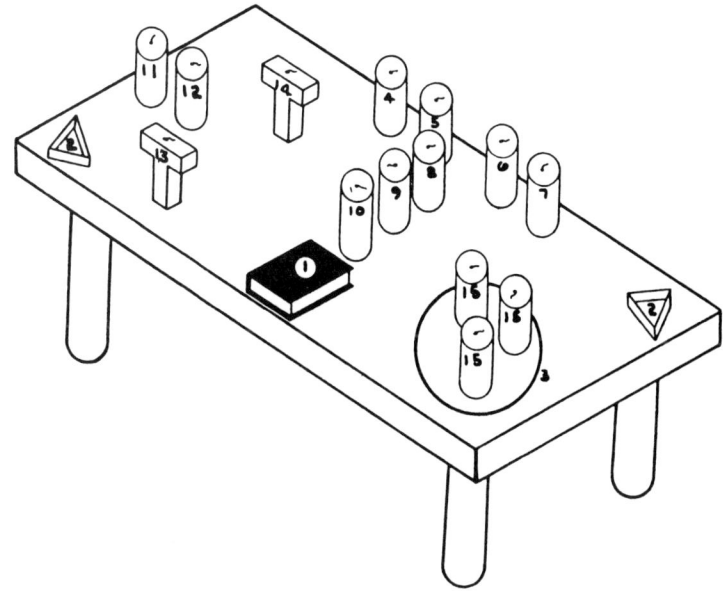

Large Group Meetings (Over Seven People)

The proper position of each item on the table or altar is as shown in the accompanying illustration. The numbers signify:

1. Bible
2. Triangular incense burners (can be any shape)
3. White chalk circle
4. Blue Spectrum Candle
5. Orange Spectrum Candle
6. Pink Spectrum Candle
7. Purple Spectrum Cundle
8. Red Spectrum Candle
9. White Spectrum Candle
10. Yellow Spectrum Candle
11. Primary Monthly Vibratory Candle
12. Secondary Monthly Vibratory Candle
13. Primary Daily Cross Candle
14. Secondary Daily Cross Candle
15. Special Purpose Cand les of varying c olors. May be three or more (as called for in subsequent chapters)

3

Seating Arrangements & Ritual Procedures

Instructions for Preparing the Worship Place

Place a saucer or small tin can almost filled with water on the floor of each room. Pour ten drops of **Rosemary Oil** in each container of water. Let them remain there in the room until the ceremony is over.

Place one **Devotional Candle** in each room. Light these candles and allow them to remain burning until they go out by themselves. Then take a bottle of **Florida Water** and carefully empty it into a basin or pail. Add two quarts of **Holy Water** and mix thoroughly. Sprinkle this mixture, with your right hand only, in each corner of every room. Then sprinkle the altar or table. While doing this, you must murmer in a low voice, the following words:

"Ezekiel, Israelis, may the blessings of God enter here. Amen."

After every room in the house has been thoroughly sprinkled, use the rest for making *protection crosses.* A protection cross is to be made on each wall of every room. Then carry the remaining water outside and go to the rear of the house, church, or place of business. Make another protection cross by the back door and under each window. Reenter the building. Proceed to the back and throw the rest of the water out of any rear window.

After all of the above steps have been completed, take some **John the Conqueror Incense** and place in a burner, or a small saucer. Light and then carry this incense through every room to be dressed

Seating Arrangements & Ritual Procedures

in preparation for a service. Return to the room from which you started and kneel in front of the burning Devotional Candle. Repeat the following prayer three times:

> "Almighty God, we beseech thee mercifully to incline shine ears to us who have now made our prayers and supplications unto thee; and grant that those things which we have faithfully asked according to thy will, may effectually be obtained to the relief of our necessity, and to the setting forth of thy glory."

Rise and take some **Lucky Nine Mixture** and sprinkle three drops in each corner of every room. This is said to allow luck to come and evil forces to leave. After this sprinkling, pick up a Bible and read **Psalm 91**. When you finish reading this Psalm, gather all the saucers or tin cans containing the **Oil of Rosemary** and water. Pour into one large bottle and go outside to the front of the house or church. Sprinkle around on the ground until it is all gone. Return to the inside of the building and kneel before the first Devotional Candle. Proceed to read **Psalm 21** from the good book. Be very careful to let the Devotional Candles burn out before moving them.

When you have done all of the above things properly, only the divine blessing must be expected. Darkness will turn to sunshine, sadness to gladness, and woe to happiness. God will be with you in the service.

PRIVATE SESSIONS (ALONE)

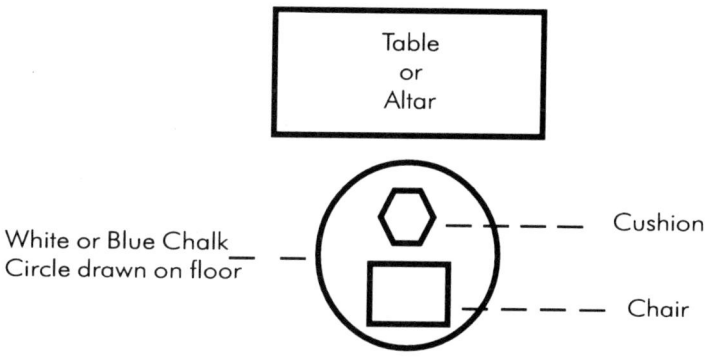

Consultation Sessions (with one other person)

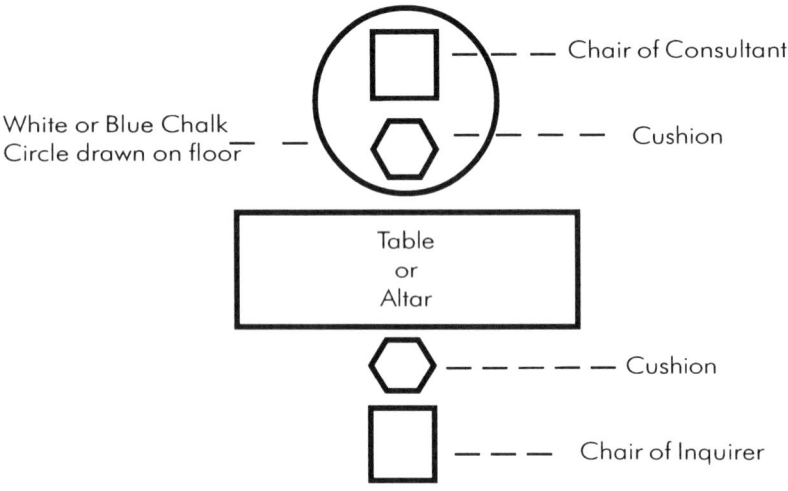

Small Group Meetings (7 people or less)

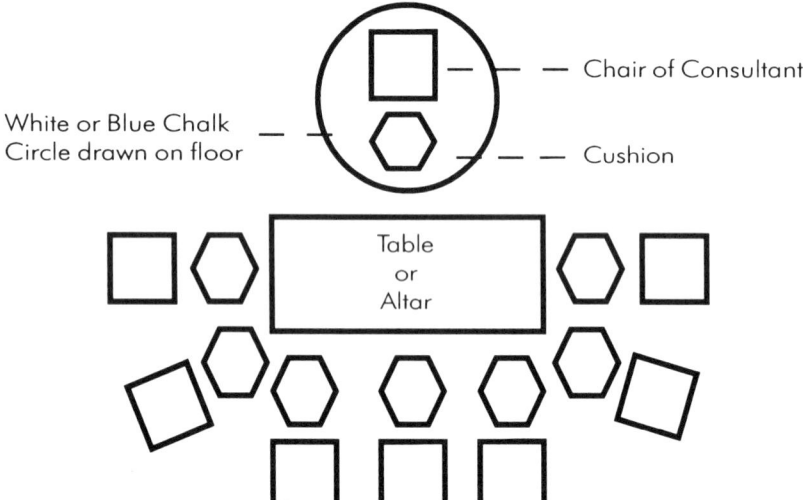

Seven Chairs to sit in and seven cushions to kneel on must be provided in the arrangement shown above.

Seating Arrangements & Ritual Procedures

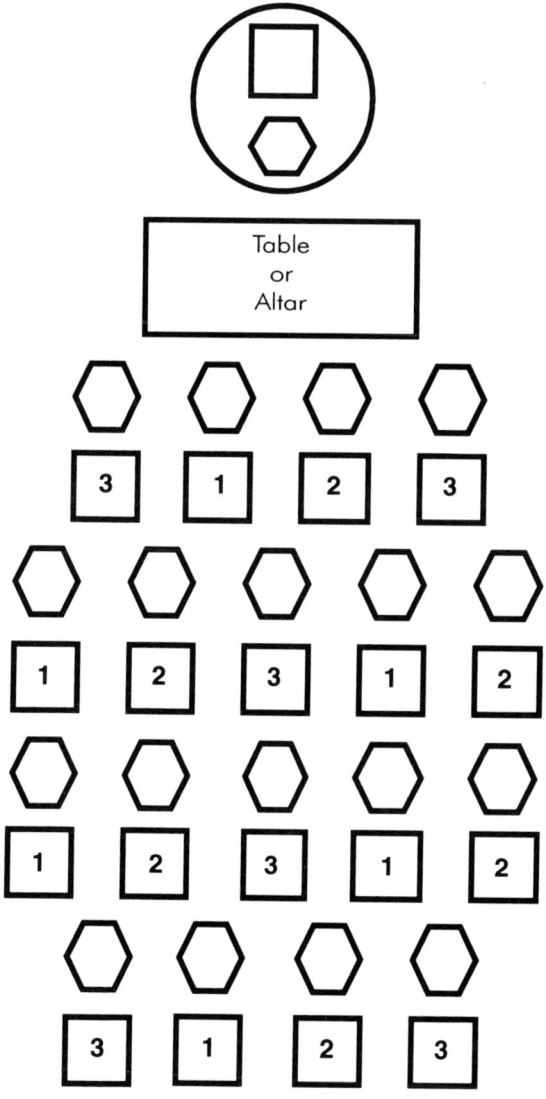

Must sit in series of three as shown above.

Large Group Meetings (over seven people)

Conducting a Proper Novena

Even before the coming of Christ this ancient religious custom has been handed down from generation to generation. It was practiced by the ancient Hebrews and is now utilized by Christians of many denominations. It is also practiced by the Chinese in a different form, and was used in ancient Egypt.

The novena consists of burning nine candles on nine different days or nights and burning one at a time. It has been asked over and over again, just what is a novena, what does it mean, and what is its objective in white magic? The word novena is from the Latin meaning "a new beginning." In other words, you leave all the old behind and begin a new life just as if you were born again. It is akin to the ressurection. Sins are left in the past as are all mistakes. The novena relieves the burdens of guilt for past misdeeds.

A novena is considered to be very powerful when used in white magic rituals. Begin by writing the wish you desire on a piece of pure parchment paper. In case you want to exert influence on a particular person, the name of that individual is to be written on the parchment paper. Use only ***Dove's Blood Ink*** for this purpose. Place the paper under each burning Devotional Candle in such a manner that the wax will drip on the paper and cover the writing.

A prayer of thanks must be given before the candle is initially lit, and another is murmured while the candle burns. The second prayer must clearly state exactly what it is the person desires to accomplish. It must be prayed for earnestly, and with fervor and piety.

Some people practice this rite by placing under the candle a photograph of the person they wish to influence. This is done in lieu of the writing on the parchment. Both of these methods work well, but the most power is gained if the name is written on parchment and included with a photograph

It is very important that no candle blow out once it has been lit. If any one of the nine do, it is a serious sign of danger - an ill omen. In such cases, whether you are burning the first candle or the ninth, the novena must begin all over again. You must stop and start a new one.

A woman can ask in a novena that her husband or lover shall come back to her. She can request all his other loves to die in him. She can force him to begin life over again with her and renew the flames of love.

So a boy can ask for understanding and assistance in his studies and his duties. He can become a success in his chosen employment and obtain the job he most desires. All old mistakes will be left behind. All the old misgivings and uncertainties will leave his mind. He can overcome all trials and tribulations.

And so can you eliminate the things you would like to forget. You can force others to forgive you and you will forgive them for past injustices. You can wipe your memory clean and start fresh. All evil will be forgotten and left behind for your benefit and peace of mind. You have a second chance at life through the all-powerful novena.

To Gain Spiritual Assistance

Arrange the table or altar as illustrated in Chapter two. Light your two Monthly Vibratory Candles, two Daily Cross Candles, and the following Special Purpose Candles: one red, one white, and one purple. Close your eyes, concentrate, and then carefully repeat this invocation:

> *"O Good Mother I come to you with tears in my eyes and a heart as heavy as steel. My whole life is full of regret for the many years that I have wasted and all of the sorrows I have undergone because of my own ignorance. All around me are others who have reaped the goodness that life has had to offer, while I have only had misery and sorrow. I beg of you Dear Mother to help me to overcome all the years that I have neglected my spiritual life. Believe me, Dear Mother, that the fault was not mine alone, as I had no one to guide me, no one to advise me. Without your help, Dear Mother, I see an endless life of hopeless sorrow. Humbly, I beg you Dear Mother, to lift me from my knees and lead me to the path of spiritual growth and everlasting hope.*
>
> *"Help me to fear no longer my Dear Mother, let happiness be within my grasp. Help me to start from the beginning to build my mind, my body, and my home to the highest possible level. And when I do these many good things, let me not forget the unhappy times and the people around*

me who still need a helping hand spiritually for each time I help another person I advance on my own ladder of happiness."

To Become a Spiritualist or Medium

Arrange the table or altar as illustrated in Chapter two. Light your two Monthly Vibratory Candles, two Daily Cross Candles, and the following Special Purpose Candles: one brown, one pink, one red, one white, and one purple. Close your eyes, concentrate, and then carefully repeat this invocation:

> "O Dear Mother, I kneel before you in a desire to gain your assistance in my time of great need. I have the desire to be of great service to others. I want to comfort and help those who come before me with supplications, tears in their eyes, a painful heart, and troubles mounting from day to day. They have no one to turn to but me. I am burdened with my own troubles in addition to the unfortunate afflictions of others.
>
> "I realize it is not an easy path in life. It is absolutely necessary that I be in complete control of all my faculties. If I truly aim to others, according to the spiritual law, I must first be strong spiritually in order that I may absorb the power so essential in the process of assisting others.
>
> "O Dear Mother help me not to worry any longer. Bring a smile of contentment to my face, and allow my great desires to come to pass. Please show me the lighted path that I might follow in order to accomplish my good and just ends."

To Gain Spiritual Strength

The history of divine revelations and the influence of the wise men is found in the Holy Scriptures. It points out the true relationship of man to the Omnipotent. And it affords the most direct reference to the great truth of the spiritual forces.

Special preparations are required to develop the spiritualist

Thank you for buying this book. If you would like to receive any further information about our product list, please return this card after filling in your areas of interest.

Title of this book..
If purchased : Retailer's name......................Town.......................

- ☐ Health and Nutrition
- ☐ Indigenous Cultures
- ☐ Occult & Divination
- ☐ Personal Growth
- ☐ Philosophy & Spirituality
- ☐ Psychology & Psychotherapy
- ☐ Women's Interest
- ☐ Other

Name..
Address..
....
....

DEEP BOOKS LTD
UNIT 3 GOOSE GREEN TRADING ESTATE
47 EAST DULWICH ROAD
LONDON
SE22 9BN
UK

AFFIX STAMP HERE

control of visions, and to properly be able to interpret dream meanings. It is of paramount importance to keep **Spirit Oil** on hand at all times. This oil is to be rubbed on your entire body at twelve midnight. Then light seven white Spiritual Candles which also have been anointed with the same **Spirit Oil.**

During the hours of meditation, let some Blessed Incense be burning on the altar or table. Mix **Dragon Blood Incense** with this to gain even further strength.

If you are conducting a white magic service of this type, and others are present, anoint everyone's entire body with **Holy Oil**. Only the consultant may do this task, and it must be accomplished prior to initiating the rites, and lighting the seven required candles. No less than seven Spiritual Candles made of pure wax should be burning during such services.

After this part of the ritual has been successfully completed, take one teaspoonful of **Vesta Powder** and place it in an incense burner or a saucer. Light with one of the seven candles. Stand back and when the flames die down, fan the fumes over your entire body. Each participant in turn, while completely nude, must follow suit.

Go into a deep meditation for one hour following the fanning of the burning **Vesta Powder** fumes. Then take one-half tablespoon of **Dragon Blood Oil** and place it in a tub of bath water. Each person in attendance is to climb into the tub, submerge completely, and immediately get out.

Now get a piece of pure parchment paper for each person. Write the **Seal Number Seven of the Sixth and Seventh Book of Moses** using only **Doves Blood Ink**. This piece of paper is then to be worn to bed. All dreams will be clearer and much more easily understood. The wearer will learn what he desires through many dreams and visions.

4

INVOCATIONS FOR LOVE AND MARRIAGE

WHEN YOUR WIFE WALKS OUT ON YOU

Arrange the table or altar as illustrated in Chapter two. Light your two Monthly Vibratory Candles, two Daily Cross Candles, and the followirig Special Purpose Candles: one red or pink, one yellow, one white, and one purple. Close your eyes, concentrate, and then carefully repeat this invocation:

"O Good Mother, look into your son's upturned face and bear with him until he has told you of his trouble and sorrow and poured his tale of misery at your feet. He comes to you for help and comfort, knowing that in all your wisdom he can count on happiness if you so wish it.

"Dear Mother, the woman of my heart has left my roof and I have no peace or rest. She has gone from me with very few words and has left me brokenhearted for I have her always in my mind and cannot sleep for her face is always before me. I cannot gain peace for the remembrance of all the times when so many sweet words were spoken to each other and so many tender moments were passed in each other's company.

"Tales have come to my ears that she has left me for another man who she loves better than she does me. Other tales are that she left because she does not love me any more, as she used to do in the long ago. I do not know what to do or

what to believe. I come to you that you might quiet my mind and make her think of me often and make her come back to me and love me in the same old way as she did before.

"Please Dear Mother, answer my brokenhearted plea in haste that I may take my rightful place again in the house of happiness, for love is at the bottom of all things and rules the world."

TO REGAIN A LOVER

Arrange the table or altar as illustrated in Chapter two. Light your two Monthly Vibratory Candles, two Daily Cross Candles, and the following Special Purpose Candles: one red or pink, one yellow, one white, and one purple. Close your eyes, concentrate, and then carefully repeat this invocation:

"O my Great Mother, I come unto you and say, Good Mother, the man of my heart has left me. He no longer comes to my house and tells me of his undying love and devotion. He passes me by without any smile on his face. His eyes no longer sparkle with love when he speaks to me. His heart is cold to all of my advances. He has eyes for other women. I have no longer the power to hold his tender thoughts. He listens to the voices of the sirens and does not hearken unto me.

"O Good Mother, I come unto you in deep distress and poor in spirit. I beg for your help that I may be comforted and loved just as in the days gone by, and that my loved one may remain by my side, for all of the beauty and sunshine has gone from my life. Please Great Mother, assist your poor downcast daughter in this time of trial. It is with deep feeling and regret that I burden you with my great pains and tribulations. But it is written that the sun shall again shine for me in gladness, and that only you can help me to accomplish this great desire."

To Become More Sexually Exciting

Arrange the table or altar as illustrated in Chapter two. Light your two Monthly Vibratory Candles, two Daily Cross Candles, and the following Special Purpose Candles: one red or pink, one yellow, one white, and one purple. Close your eyes, concentrate, and then carefully repeat this invocation:

> "O Good Mother, I pray you to judge me and give me some much needed advice, for my men friends do not smile on me. They meet me and see me not, they do not speak to me in the warm words of love and friendship, they forget me even as I pass, they do not even remember my name. When I go to a party I sit near the wall unadorned and uncalled for. They have no bright sayings for me and care not to incur my favor so I remain forlorn and forsaken while all about me is laughter and good fellowship. Lo, I am with them but not of them.
>
> When I speak to them and ask them to come to my house and visit me, neither do they say yes, nor do they say no. If they come they make no effort to entertain me, nor to make me carefree or mirthful. They speak to me only in a cool and distant manner.
>
> "Dear Mother, hear my words of trouble and sympathize with me. Make my bright star shine again and relieve my mind of all tension and anxiety. Allow me to be more seductive and alluring. Turn me into a sensual woman that no friend will be able to resist. Please Mother Dear, make those who ignore me now soon desire me as an animal desires another. Force them to feel the fires of passion on looking at me when we meet. Only you, can bring such strength to bear in this heart rending problem."

To Gain Peace in the Home

Arrange the table or altar as illustrated in Chapter two. Light your two Monthly Vibratory Candles, two Daily Cross Candles, and the following Special Purpose Candles: one light blue, one orange, one white, and one purple. Close your eyes, concentrate, and then carefully repeat this invocation:

"My Mother and friend, I come unto you with tears in my eyes and deeply worried over the condition of my home. Where there should be harmony, love, understanding, and peace, only sadness and disappointment fill the atmosphere. I need your advice Dear Mother of All Things, and I will faithfully follow your instructions and bring sunshine into my home. And in my house there shall be no evil thoughts. In my house there shall only be cheerfulness. And I will keep this spirit of cheer in my house by scrubbing the floors with water in which a few drops of Van Van Floor Wash have been mixed.

'O Dear Mother, I will do all things you might ask of me, and I will let no frown be reflected on my face. I know you will use your great powers to help and comfort me at this time. I kneel before you with tears in my eyes, and an aching heart. My troubles have mounted and I am burdened with the problems of dissatisfaction in my home. Please Dear Mother, come to your poor daughters rescue now. I beg of you to relieve me of such unhappiness."

TO HELP FIND A NEW SWEETHEART

Arrange the table or altar as illustrated in Chapter two. Light your two Monthly Vibratory Candles, two Daily Cross Candles, and the following Special Purpose Candles: one red or pink, one yellow, one white, and one purple. Close your eyes, concentrate, and then carefully repeat this invocation:

"O Dear Mother, I come unto you so that I can get some of your good and wholesome advice for I don't seem to have any luck or any chance to get a sweetheart. I see them and speak sweetly to them and they seem to like my looks and they harken unto my words. But lo when I go back the second time all of their encouragement seems to have gone. I meet them at parties and seem to have a very good time with them and make them joyous and happy, but when I speak of calling upon them they immediately turn a deaf ear unto me.

"O Mother I meet them socially and in company and

seem to be welcome, but when I wish to communicate with them privately, lo their excuses are many and I can make no headway in my love affairs. O my Good Mother my heart yearns for the love of a sweetheart. It would be my complete happiness if I could make them better un derstand me and make them love and sexually desire me in return.

"Please Mother Dear, tell me, oh tell me, what ha. done this to me. When all of my friends are successful in conquest I am to be cast off and can find no place and no one to give my caresses to and talk of sweet love to. Mother, I am glad I came unto you and am asking your advice and seeking your direction. Many other of your good sons are beset with this same evil yet they come not to you for assistance and guidance. I seem to be surrounded with the spirit of opposition and cannot make my way with the one I would love. Only you can give me the proper instructions so that I might be blessed with the good spirits. I will do all things you say to get the help of the God of Love, so that he will give me many happy days."

WHEN YOUR HUSBAND LEAVES

Arrange the table or altar as illustrated in Chapter two. Light your two Monthly Vibratory Candles, two Daily Cross Candles, and the following Special Purpose Candles: one red or pink, one yellow, one white, and one purple. Close your eyes, concentrate, and then carefully repeat this invocation:

"O Good Mother, I come unto you in deep distress. Tears have coursed my face in the dark hours of the night for he who was flesh of my flesh, the blood of my heart, and the companion of my soul. My dear husband has left our home and gone from my side. He has gone into the wilderness where my cries of distress will not reach him, where my tender words will not lie heard by him, where the sirens and the bad women will have sway over him and will make him forget me forever. He is gone where I cannot minister unto him, where I cannot show my love and devotion. He has left me desolate and where darkness closes in and about me and drags me

down to the depths of hell.

"O Good Mother, I cannot possibly live without him. I am sorely pressed and ask only for death without your help. O Mother of mine, I will not lose hope and faith with you by my side for the stars say that there is a way to make my loved one's spirit communicate with me. You can guide him back to my side, there to remain and to comfort and protect me. Please Good Mother, bring my problem to the attention of the good spirits and get their help for me. Ask the good spirits to stop the work of the spirits of ill-omen against me, so that I will again find happiness."

TO REGAIN HAPPINESS IN LOVE

Arrange the table or altar as illustrated in Chapter two. Light your two Monthly Vibratory Candles, two Daily Cross Candles, and the following Special Purpose Candles: one blue, one orange, one white, and one purple. Close your eyes, concentrate, and then carefully repeat this invocation:

"O Good Mother, I come unto you with my heart bowed down and my shoulders drooping and my spirit broken, for an enemy has sorely tried me. They have caused my loved one to leave me, have taken from my worldly goods and of my money, have spoken meanly of me, and caused my friends to lose faith in me. The power of evil is great in my life.

"On my knees I pray to you O Good Mother that you will cause confusion to reign in my enemy's house and that you will cause hatred to be on my enemy's head and that you will take their power from them and cause them to be unsuccessful.

"O Great Mother, hear my tales of woe, and my pains and tribulations. In the depth of the wisdom of the Gods I beg of you to assist me in finding peace and happiness. I will abide by your every instruction so that I may control my enemies and take all of the power to harm me away from them. I will go in peace and do whatever you require of me so that I may have rest and comfort from my enemies. I know that with your help they will no longer have any

power to harm me in the sight of my friends and loved ones by their stinging tongues."

When You Lose a Sweetheart

Arrange the table or altar as illustrated in Chapter two. Light your two Monthly Vibratory Candles, two Daily Cross Candles, and the following Special Purpose Candles: one red or pink, one yellow, one white, and one purple. Close your eyes, concentrate, and then carefully repeat this invocation:

"O Dear Mother, you see your son before you with tears in his eyes and a downcast look in his face for I have lost my beautiful sweetheart whom I have loved for many a day and whom I cannot possibly soon forget. She is always in my mind and I cannot sleep for the thoughts of her even during the day time. In my fancy I see her just out of my reach. Her beautiful form and face is always before me, night and day, in all my waking hours and in my hours of labor.

"I see no more her sweet smile when she received me. I hear not her sweet voice when she spoke to me. I would gladly give half my life for another moment of happiness with her such as there were so many before. O Mother will you hear my prayer and help me? I am your poor son who needs some sign that you hearken to my words of sorrow. Please extend me your help that I may smile again the smile of happiness and that I will again be glad to see the streak of daylight break the skies. Comfort me that my tears will stop flowing and I will be myself again with my sweetheart at my side.

"Lo. In order to bring about this great day, I will do exactly as you say unto me. When I come upon my sweetheart again, she will smile and speak to me words of endearment and make me a happy person."

5

INVOCATIONS TO DRAW GOOD FORTUNE

TO OBTAIN GENERAL SUCCESS

Arrange the table or altar as illustrated in Chapter two. Light your two Monthly Vibratory Candles, two Daily Cross Candles, and the following Special Purpose Candles: one orange, one yellow, one white, and one purple. Close your eyes, concentrate, and then carefully repeat this invocation:

> *"O Dear Mother, I come unto you to ask for your help. My mind and my spirit have been burdened to the breaking point. I beg of thee, O Dear Mother, to turn no deaf ears to my supplications that I may be successful in those things which I desire within the bounds of reason.*
>
> *"O Dear Mother, I plead with thee to understand my tribulations and trials. Please show me the path that I might take in order to accomplish the desires of my heavily burdened heart. Hear my pleas! Hear my pleas! Hear my pleas!"*

TO QUICKLY GAIN NEW FRIENDSHIPS

Arrange the table or altar as illustrated in Chapter two. Light your two Monthly Vibratory Candles, two Daily Cross Candles, and the following Special Purpose Candles: one blue, one yellow, one white, and one purple. Close your eyes, concentrate, and then carefully repeat this invocation:

"O Good Mother, the evil spirit seems to completely envelop me in this dire hour. I have no attraction powers, no sympathy from any of my kind. All my former friends look upon me with a great deal of indifference. Their friendship and love is no more than a slight lukewarm. Their former understanding has fled. And their once strong interest in me as a human being has waned.

"O Mother Dear, I ask these people for favors and they promise, but they never do as I request of them. I invite them in and they say yes, but none ever comes to visit me. They pass me in the market place and sometimes acknowledge my physical presence, but more often they look me not in the face. They stop and speak to others, but when I approach there is no more to speak about and everything becomes very quiet.

"Mother, O Mother, I seem to have lost the power to hold my friendships. They look upon me with their eyes and they see me not. They speak with their lips, but their words are empty and of no consequence or value. O Great Mother, please help me to regain my truly lost spirit. Make my words to friends ring true, so they will again believe me. Restore my magnetism so all of my actions will attract others to me always. Help me to look well into myself first and take heed that I try to better value my true friends. Please Dear One called Mother, Allow me to have more of the great power of attraction. Give me this loving strength once again."*

To Develop Happiness

Arrange the table or altar as illustrated in Chapter two. Light your two Monthly Vibratory Candles, two Daily Cross Candles, and the following Special Purpose Candles: one blue, one orange, one purple, and one white. Close your eyes, concentrate, and then carefully repeat this invocation:

"O Dear Mother, I plead with you to help me to better understand the importance of self-sacrifice on my long journey through this life. Help me, O Good Mother, to attain the highest possible degree of bliss and happiness. Teach me to walk through the harsh valley of suffering and to better *stand the pain and misfortune of my mind and body.*

"Mother O Mother, assist your humble servant in learning how to control these important things, for I realize this is the ultimate in learning to live right. O Dear Mother, show me the most effective way to accomplish this most sincere purpose in my life. I promise to always remember that the darkest hour is just before the dawn of day. I promise to do all things good, Dear Mother, and to let the sunshine of happiness enter fully into my new birth."

TO POWERFULLY INFLUENCE OTHERS

Arrange the table or altar as illustrated in Chapter two. Light your two Monthly Vibratory Candles, two Daily Cross Candles, and the following Special Purpose Candles: one brown, one pink, one purple, and one white. Close your eyes, concentrate, and then carefully repeat this invocation:

"My Dear Mother, I come unto you because I sincerely seek out your all powerful assistance. I have been devoid of the power to influence those with whom I come into contact. It is written, I know, Dear Mother, that to follow your instructions is to accomplish any of my desires. This I will do without question.

"O Great Mother, I know how important it is that my body be clean at all times. And so too with my raiment. I seek your guidance and your power with great faith and I ask God to help me through you. Assist me gracious one, for I am now seeking in desperation. I am full of need at this time.

"I will, O Mother Dear, on the fifth day of every week, which is called Friday, upon arising, recite this prayer:

'O Lord God Almighty, be Thou favorable unto me, though I am unworthy to lift my eyes to heaven by reason of the multitude of my past offenses. O God all-merciful, who wiliest not the death of a sinner, but rather his true conversion, bestow Thy grace upon me! O Lord, O God, full of compassion, aid me in this hour of need and grant me my desire that Thy name may be blessed forever. Amen.'

"After doing this, O Mother Dear, I shall go forth to the new day and do all that I possibly can that is clean and good. I will have no fear but that I will receive my divine aid."

To Accomplish Your Goals

Arrange the table or altar as illustrated in Chapter two. Light your two Monthly Vibratory Candles, two Daily Cross Candles, and the following Special Purpose Candles: one yellow, one orange, one purple, and one white. Close your eyes, concentrate, and then carefully repeat this invocation:

"O Great Mother, sometimes it seems as though everything is against me. Whatever I attempt to do turns in the opposite direction. I find it very difficult to find a way to straighten my life out. O Dear Mother, please assist me in this grave time of disorder and need.

"O Good Mother, When I almost reach my goal or my special desire, something always seems to happen to upset and block my progress. Things I am reaching for disappear into nothing. All of this creates strife and sorrow and leaves me in a perpetual state of want and despair. Help me, Dear Mother, to take these reverses with more calm and more faith. Fill my empty heart with hope for things better. God bless you, O Mother Dear, for you are good to me when I am in need."

How to Get a Good Job

Arrange the table or altar as illustrated in Chapter two. Light your two Monthly Vibratory Candles, two Daily Cross Candles, and the following Special Purpose Candles: one orange, one yellow, one light green, one white, and one purple. Close your eyes, concentrate, and then carefully repeat this invocation:

"O Dear Mother, I come to you with a supplication which I pray you will see fit to grant me. I find myself at a

complete loss and have no one to whom I can turn for help. Whenever I find myself where I think I am doing well, the evil spirits surrounding me seem to interfere with my progress. I seem to always find myself in debt with my closest friends.

"O Good Mother, at this time my difficulties grow to the point that I wish I lived no longer. Therefore, I humbly beg of thee, Dear Mother, to help me in this dire time of need. I will forever be grateful to you all the remaining years of my life.

"I know, Dear Mother, you hesitate not in your feelings of sympathy for me in my darkest hour. I will not give up hope for I know there is always a Big Almighty who watches over me twenty-four hours each day. I also know He will not overburden me with more than my frail body can stand.

"Mother, O Dear Mother, I realize it is the strong in spirit who finally attain the good wishes and blessings of God. I promise to go forth and make the necessary application for the job I most desire. I will carry with me the good recommendation of my former employer. I promise you I will not stop on my first attempt, but will keep on striving. I know you are sending the good and powerful spirits to help me most of the way along this perilous path.

"Yes, O Mother Dear, I will stop fretting and worrying. I will keep a good smile on my face knowing my desire will soon come to pass. Thank you Mother, O Great Mother. I promise to keep our pact a carefully guarded secret in order that you may better control the good spiritual forces surrounding me, and so these spirits will not divide their rapt attention."

To Hold a Job Under All Circumstances

Arrange the table or altar as illustrated in Chapter two. Light Your two Monthly Vibratory Candles, two Daily Cross Candles, and the following Special Purpose Candles: one orange, one yellow, one purple, and one white. Close your eyes, concentrate, and then carefully repeat this invocation:

"O Gracious Mother, I come to you with a clean heart and a clear desire for the ultimate perfection I know only you can possibly give me. Fear is gradually taking possession of my soul and slowly consuming my vitality. At times I do not know whether my steps lead me forward or backward. At times my boss looks upon me with scorn and disdain. At other times he showers me with kindness and favors.

"O Mother Dear, all of this makes me believe the evil spirits are working against me. I feel these evil spirits all around me on this job I now have and which I would especially like to keep. But everything seems to be gently slipping out from under me feet. Can I not be more secure?

"Now Dear Mother, I beg of you to help me keep my position around which I have built all my future hopes. I believe both the good and the evil spirits are working for and against me. I have neglected to do the things I should have done in harmony with the good spirits and to help destroy the evil ones.

"I will bow to your commands, O Mother, so you may help me to eliminate the spirit of gloom that constantly hovers over my head. Push away this evil force which leaves me in a never ending uncertain state of mind. I shall never again allow frowns appear on my face as this tends to draw more of the spirits of evil. I shall never think gloomily as this makes it more difficult for the good spirits to do their wonderful work for God the Father.

"I now say the following special prayer, O Mother Dear, and I promise to faithfully repeat this prayer, at bedtime, for seven successive nights:

'O Great and living God, who has created man to enjoy felicity in this life; who has adopted all things for man's necessity; and didst declare that everything should be made subject to his will. Be favorable to this, my prayer, and permit not the evil spirits to be in possession of my body and my soul. Grant me, O Great Lord God, the power to dispose of these evil spirits through Your help. I will forever remain Thy faithful and obedient servant. Amen.'"

To Change Your Luck

Arrange the table or altar as illustrated in Chapter two. Light your two Monthly Vibratory Candles, two Daily Cross Candles, and the following Special Purpose Candles: one yellow, one purple, and one white. Close your eyes, concentrate, and then carefully repeat this invocation:

"O Good Mother, I come unto you to lay at your feet my most deep troubles. It seems everything I may try to do goes against me. When I think I have something with which I can quickly gather pieces of gold and wax fat and prosperous, lo, it is but clay in my hands. I can get no encouragement from the women and men with whom I speak. I am always turned a deaf ear so they will not bother to even hear me. When I see a place in which I might succeed, and put my cash into it, lo, the customers do not come. They seem to pass my door and do not even bother to look around.

"Mother, Dear Mother, I often see good merchandise and good chattels I can pick up cheaply, and then sell them at much profit. Lo, when they come into my hands they are only dross and have no value. I go to see the big chiefs and talk pleasantly to them. I explain how I can do many things to their advantage, and will make them wax fat with riches. Lo, they turn their heads and will not listen to my humble words.

"So it is, O Dear Mother, one failure after another, one disappointment after another. Here I am on my knees before you with very few shekels and a very poor heart. My spirit is broken and I know not what to do. Will you, O Good Mother, also turn me away empty-handed and leave me in despair? I pray in hopes that you will see fit to call upon the good spirits to assist me, and that you will take me as your own.

"I will rise up, O Mother, and take heart, for I know those stout of courage and with willing hands cannot possibly fail. You will not, O Mother Dear, let me again fail even if the evil spirits have conspired against me. Lend me your gracious hands and your unselfish assistance. Uphold me and make me great and strong again. I now recite the following prayer,

O Great Mother, and promise you faithfully to repeat it at bedtime for seven successive nights:

> '*Oh Good Lord, make me stouter of heart.*
> *Oh Good Lord, let my sight penetrate the innermost secrets of success.*
> *Oh Good Lord, give me the power to speak clearly.*
> *Oh Good Lord, let others hearken to my words.*
> *Oh Good Lord, drive all evil spirits away from me.*
> *Oh Good Lord, give me the success I desire most.*
> *Oh Good Lord, allow me to hold on to all these good things in my life.*
> *Oh Good Lord, never again leave your faithful follower and believer.*'

"*Mother Dear, I know this short prayer is the great secret of my coming successes. My luck, through your power, is destined to radically reverse itself. I will carefully write this prayer on parchment and keep it with me always, to look at, and to read, and to cherish above all else. I know you will give me power and more confidence in myself. I know I can now go forth without anymore fear and hesitation. All things good must come to me and I shall no longer know any such word as failure and distress.*"

6

Invocations to Gain Financially

When Good Luck Evades You

Arrange the table or altar as illustrated in Chapter 2. Light your two Monthly Vibratory Candles, two Daily Cross Candles, and the following Special Purpose Candles: one yellow, one orchid, one white, and one purple. Close your eyes, concentrate, and then carefully repeat this invocation:

> *"O my Dear Mother, your child comes to you with tears in the eyes and a downcast look in the face. I have lost all that I ever possessed in this world. My hopes are fast vanishing and I have no one to turn to but you. I therefore, O Mother, implore you to aid me. Restore to me the smile and happiness that was once mine. I would give part of my life for some better luck, the kind of luck I used to possess.*
>
> *"O Mother, will jots hear my supplication and offer to help me? Listen to my words of sorrow and gladly give your assistance that I may again be fortunate and blissful. Please, O Great Mother, lend me the help I so desperately require."*

To Increase Your Finances

Arrange the table or altar as illustrated in Chapter 2. Light your two Monthly Vibratory Candles, two Daily Cross Candles, and the following Special Purpose Candles: one light green, one dark green, one purple, and one white. Close your eyes concentrate, and then carefully repeat this invocation:

> "O Good Mother, I come to you to request your help, for prosperity and plenty is not for me. The stranger passes my door and sees me not. Neither do they stop and look into my house. My place is always empty and there is no laughter nor are there any good feast days. People know me not, on the dark days nor on the feast days. Neither do they remember me on good or bad days. I am almost always ignored.
>
> "O Mother Dear, the clink of gold has not passed my palm for many days. Neither friends nor strangers have brought me gifts. My purse hangs limp from my tassel (my wallet stays void of paper money) with no hopes of having it filled.
>
> "O Good Mother, I am full of lamentations and the evil spirits live throughout my abode. I beg that you shall hear my patient prayer and in the fullness of your wisdom alive me help. I am but one of your poor helpless children who desires only the fullness of your heart to make prosperity again smile upon me. Please help, O Mother, and allow me to again have many good feast days. Make friends remember me always and be at my side. Make my raiment be of many hues and of fine texture and let this reflect my prosperity.
>
> "I pray to you, O Mother Dear, so that all these things will come to pass soon. Let the opposite sex enter and be entertained by me. Let them remain pleased with me. Let them shower me with kindness and worldly goods. Let prosperity enter my home and drive away all care and worry. Allow the good spirits to rule my life from this day forward and I will never again question your powers. So be it."

To Become More Prosperous

Arrange the table or altar as illustrated in Chapter 2. Light your two Monthly Vibratory Candles, two Daily Cross Candles, and the following Special Purpose Candles: one light green, one dark green, one purple, and one white. Close your eyes, concentrate, and then carefully repeat this invocation:

INVOCATIONS TO GAIN FINANCIALLY

"O Dear Mother, I full know the spirit is all powerful in my life. I believe the Creator is concrete and real. I full realize the law of mankind is always the proper and ethical way to follow. These include: morality and conscience; good humor; fair play and decency; consideration; respect; altruism; faith; goodness; benevolence; and sacrifice.

"Dear Mother, O Great One, prosperity can be mine if you should hear my plea and decide to rule favorably toward me. I realize it must be purchased with fortitude and tenacity. Patience is also very important in my strenuous trek to a more prosperous life.

"I promise, O Grand Mother of All, to stay out of too much debt. I will not be a slave to my dreams and ambitions. I will sincerely try harder to save and protect my future income Give me luck, O Mother, to assist me on this climb to betterment and great successes."

TO DRAW MORE BUSINESS

Arrange the table or altar as illustrated in Chapter 2. Light your two Monthly Vibratory Candles, two Daily Cross Candles, and the following Special Purpose Can dies: one light-green, one yellow, one purple, and one white. Close your eyes, concentrate, and then carefully repeat this invocation:

"O Good Mother, your daughter (son) comes to you on bended knees to ask for a great favor. For where there was light and laughter, now there is only silence. Where many feet wore out the threshold of my front door, now scarcely anyone ever enters my humble abode.

"Mother Dear, where gold crossed my palm in a steady stream, not even a shekel is now seen. No gold, no silver, no jewels, no worldly goods come to me as before. My goods remain in my storehouse, with no one to buy or even ask me the price thereof. Is there no hope, O Great Mother?

"So Good Mother, if I do not soon get help from you I will face complete ruination. If you decide to ignore my pleaful supplication the sheriff and his minions will soon enter my household and my storehouse and take from me what I have left to sell.

"O My Mother of Goodness, it is said that she (he) who has, more again shall be given. So please make this come to pass in my humble life. Make the good spirits enter my goods so that the stranger will buy from me that which I have to sell. Or make the good spirits increase the business for me and allow more money to again pass through the palms of my hands. Do not disallow your servant such a small request.

"Thank you, O Grand One, for making prosperity again smile upon me. Strangers and friends will now come to me and say, "Lo, I am much pleased with you and I will surely come and see you again. Let the music begin for I am much satisfied in my business dealings with you."

To Gain Gambling Luck

Arrange the table or altar as illustrated in Chapter 2. Light your two Monthly Vibratory Candles, two Daily Cross Candles, and the following Special Purpose Candles: one dark green, one yellow, one purple, and one white. Close your eyes, concentrate, and then carefully repeat this invocation:

"Great Goddess of Chance, I would beg you for favor. I would ask for pieces of gold and of silver from your guiding hands. For when I go to the races the horses do not heed me or make strong efforts that I may be victor. The rider or the driver of the chariot does not lash his steed that they may come on the first line. But instead, the horses I play seem to ever lag behind and force me to lose my gold and silver.

"When I pray to you, Great Goddess of Chance, with dice in my hands, you do not ever smile upon me. Neither do you guide the dice that they may show a smiling face to me. But instead you guide them that they may turn to help the other players. I sorrowfully go home with my pockets empty and my heart heavy with sorrowful thoughts.

"So again, Great Goddess of Chance, when I sit me down among the select men and play with them the game of cards. You do not put into my hands the cards which will undo my opponents. But instead you put into the hand of the other players the high cards which will make them my masters.

"Tell me, O Great Goddess of Chance, what can I do to help appease your obvious anger and to win your approving smile of better fortune? Tell me what can I do to wax fat and have unto my purse the bright gold and jingling silver of the world? I am your steadfast worshipper and sincerely desire to win your utmost favor. I only ask of thee that my chosen horses shall come to the winner's line first; that the dice I toss will be more friendly to me; that the high cards shall burn to get into my hands.

"Great Goddess of Chance, I have asked an important favor of thee. I am burning John the Conqueror Incense at your altar and I am burning the proper candles as an offering to your kindly spirit. I know you look only with favor upon those who are your most studious worshippers. You look with disfavor upon those who come only for a day, and you know them not. Neither do you smile on them. But for those such as myself, who always worship at your shrine, you never cease to smile upon them. I am of good spirits and you love me for my intense devotion to you Therefore, Great Goddess, I wish to receive your favor. I will not fail you in this life for I want simply to enjoy more good luck and happiness."

TO IMPROVE YOUR BUSINESS

Arrange your table or altar as illustrated in Chapter 2. Light your two Monthly Vibratory Candles, two Daily Candles, and the following Special Purpose Candle one light-green, one yellow, one purple, and one white. Close your eyes, concentrate, and then carefully repeat this invocation:

"O Dear Mother, I pray you will come to my rescue I am almost to my last resort and down to my last shekel. All of my good business is gone from me. My pockets are no more heavy with the gold and silver like the olden days. My friends of past years who at one time came to me and were more than pleased with my goods are now gone from me. They pass my door and do not bother to look inside.

"Mother Dear, all those who were once glad to bid

me time and eagerly take my advice when they were in need of my goods, now believe me not. Once in a while when a stranger steps into my house of business it seems if I cannot please them with my merchandise or with words of friendship. Lo, they always walk out empty handed"

"Dear Mother, there was once gay laughter and once by pieces of silver changed hands. Now I hear only dread silence. My goods remain on the shelves until they spoiled. I cannot even get what the merchant prince asked me to pay for these things. So, Good Mother, if I do not soon get your assistance and if you do not bring once more the tinkle of silver to my purse, I will set upon by the moneylenders and the police people. Only woe will be my lot and gone will be my house of business. Good Mother, I can only turn to you for help. Pray hear my sorrowful cries of distress.

Your faithful child has sent you his (her) plea. I do sincerely believe that the glory of the Gods of Mammon surely aid me during this time of need. The Gods Mammon, through you O Mother, will surely show me the ways of good business and many customers. Please make some of my old customers come back to me and do business as they once did in the past years. I promise to continually pacify the Gods of Mammon by burning these same candles for seven minutes on seven successive nights at sundown.

"I also promise, O Good and Great Mother, to treat all my customers with due consideration and with honesty. I promise to always have kindness in my heart and showing on my face so customers will come unto me and give me their confidence and ultimate respect. I will fail you not, O Grand Mother, for I know the Gods of Mammon will not continue smiling upon me and give me gold and silver if I am not faithful and if I do not believe in their supreme power. For Mother of Greatness and Power, I fully realize that the Gods of Mammon have two heads and can easily speak both good and evil at the same time. Do not ignore my plea, Gracious Mother of All, for this servant of yours is in bad distress."

TO IMPROVE YOUR GENERAL CONDITIONS

Arrange the table or altar as illustrated in Chapter two. Light your two Monthly Vibratory Candles, two Daily Cross Candles, and the following Special Purpose Candles: one light-green, one yellow, one orchid, one white, and one purple. Close your eyes, concentrate, and then carefully repeat this invocation:

"Mother, O Great Mother, things do not seem to ever move in the direction I most seriously desire. I have made many efforts to advance without any good results. No doubt there is a cross impeding all my progress in this life. I know that you can hastily remove this obstacle by getting right at the root of my many problems. Please, O Great One, help your most humble servant for I suspect someone is holding me back intentionally and with much malice in their heart. And I suspect some kind of psychic phenomena is blocking my way to the good things I desire.

"I plead with you, O Mother Dear, to assist your downtrodden child in this time of dire consequence. I can do no more alone, I can move nowhere without your help. But I can do all with your guiding hand of spiritual light. I believe in you and your phenomenal powers. I believe in your ultimate love, strength, and wholesome goodness I shall rise from here and go my way with luck and peace. So be it"

7

INVOCATIONS FOR OVERCOMING EVIL

TO STOP GOSSIP AND SLANDER

Arrange the table or altar as illustrated in Chapter two. Light your two Monthly Vibratory Candles, two Daily Cross Candles, and the following Special Purpose Candles: one orchid, one white, and one purple. Close your eyes, concentrate, and then carefully repeat this invocation:

> "O Good Mother, I am now before you that you may fairly judge, for my friends have spoken my name from the housetops and from the hills and have attacked my character and questioned my virtue. They have spoken jealous things of me and caused my name to become a byword among the people.
>
> "O Good Mother, I now have to hang my head when I pass the friend or the stranger for I know the viper's tongue has reached them. Scandal and untruths have been called to their attention, and they have heard many dark stories and low sayings about me. Tears are in my eyes and my lips tremble.
>
> "O Mother of everything good, help your most humble servant and devotee who now worships at your shrine. Cure my aching heart and take the greatest pity upon me. Make the flush of pride brighten my cheeks and laughter come into my eyes once again where there are now only tears. Help me to walk with my head unbowed and to look all straight in the face."

To Overcome Suffering

Arrange the table or altar as illustrated in Chapter two. Light your two Monthly Vibratory Candles, two Daily Cross Candles, and the following Special Purpose Candles: one red, one orchid, one white, and one purple. Close your eyes, concentrate, and then carefully repeat this invocation:

"O Dear Mother, I come to you with tears in my eyes and weak from the pains that I have suffered through the tragic black magic work of my enemies. The evil spell cast upon me by their ill-intent has caused me untold amounts of mental and material torture. They have kept me awake nights when I should have been sleeping. They have tired me out when I should have been well rested. They have made me worry when I should have been enjoying peace and harmony. They have made me cry when I should have been smiling. They have taken away from me everything on which I have depended for happiness.

"O Dear Mother, I come unto you for assistance in helping to reverse unto them the same evil spirit that they have cast upon me. Please, O Great One, render them helpless to again hurt and harm me and others who may one day fall victim of these horrible evil forces spirits. Make them suffer as they have made me suffer.

"O Mother, I come unto you in my darkest hour of trouble. Although the spirit of revenge is not one to trifle with and is not very pleasant to handle, help me as a gesture of self-defense. Let those who have cast me the spell of evil also suffer. Let them receive the agony through which I have been and let it serve as a lesson to them."

To Rid Yourself of Evil Thoughts

Arrange the table or altar as illustrated in Chapter two. Light your two Monthly Vibratory Candles, two Daily Cross Candles, and the following Special Purpose candles: one pink, one brown, one orchid, one white, and one purple. Close your eyes, concentrate, and then fully repeat this invocation:

> "O Good Mother, the evil thoughts seem to completely surround and devour me. During the hours when I should be enjoying happiness and should be having the mental comfort which rightfully belongs to me, I find the pressure of my evil thinking is more than I can possibly bear. Day and night these evil shadows hang over me like a dark cloud from which no light is to be expected. Everything I undertake with good intentions never materializes and good fortune which was once mine has disappeared. No matter how hard I try to regain my happiness and peace of mind, there are always the same evil thoughts blocking all progress.
>
> "Dear Mother, every time I feel satisfied that everything is going well and I am about to receive and accomplish, that which I desire most, it seems something gets between me and my goodness. I can then go no further. I am always finding myself in the exact same condition as I was when I started. Therefore, I come to you Dear Mother, to beg your help and your power for overcoming the tremendous influence of evil over my life. These evil thoughts are in complete control of me and I know not which way to turn. Please, O Dear Mother, help me to be happy and full of contentment once more.
>
> "O My Mother, I come unto you in this hour of trouble so you may bless me and assist me in acquiring the bliss, sunshine, and good fortune that was once mine. Everything has now been taken away by the evil thoughts created by the jealousy and envy of those who pretend to my friends. Let my plea touch you deeply, O Great Mother, for truly it is most pitiful that a bleeding heart, yearning for help, knows not which way to turn. I am sorely groping for your assistance and understanding to help free me from fear and uncertainty."

To Stop Legal Persecution

Arrange the table or altar as illustrated in Chapter two. Light your two Monthly Vibratory Candles, two Daily Cross Candles, and the following Special Purpose Candles: one dark blue, one orchid, one white, and one purple. Close your eyes, concentrate, and then carefully repeat this invocation:

"*O Good Mother, I am on my knees before you to pray for assistance as I am deeply troubled and I am being persecuted by my enemies. They say unto the judge, 'lo, this woman (man) has broken the law. She (he) has made war on us and caused disturbances in our family.' Another one says, 'O most learned judge, this woman (man) has taken weapons of war and has tried to spill my life's blood.' And still yet another says to the High Sheriff, 'O Sir, I pray for you to help me for this woman (man) has taken my worldly goods. She (he) has entered my house when I was away doing my labor.'*

"*O Good Mother, now the learned judge and the high sheriff and the men of the law have threatened to put me in the dungeon, the jail. It has no light and the vermin will crawl over me and eat out my heart. Only gloom will be my companion. And I will never again see the beautiful face of the sun. O Good Mother, help your poor downtrodden daughter (son).*

"*O Great Mother, hear my prayer and hasten to help me with heartfelt sympathy. Tell me the secrets of the learned judges and the men of law so I may conquer my enemies. Let me once more, O Mother Dear, breathe the fresh air of freedom. Allow the rays of the sun to shine brightly upon my head and bring me comfort and peace of mind. Make the good moon bring a smile to my trouble wracked face.*

"*O Mother of Creation, make the testimony of my enemies not be believed by the learned judge. Force her (him) to become confused when she (he) speaks to the judge against me. You can, O Dear One, do all of these things so I may triumph over my enemies and have more power and blissfulness.*"

To Control Troublemakers

Arrange the table or altar as illustrated in Chapter two Light your two Monthly Vibratory Candles, two Daily Cross Candles, and the following Special Purpose Candles: one pink, one brown, one orchid, on white, and one purple. Close your eyes, concentrate, and then carefully repeat this invocation:

"O Dear Mother, I come unto you to tell you of my unsettled mind and of my most grave troubles. There is someone who lives near me, but who has no neighborly love for me nor for anyone else. This bad person is only full of selfishness and is of a very mean turn of mind. He (she) makes continual trouble and distress for everyone who lives close to me and around me. There is constant strife and loud wailing wherever that person may be when I pass near his (her) place of living, he (she) at once utters vicious words loud enough so these words will reach my ears. He (she) does this in order that I may stop and say to them mean words in return. This, O Mother, surely will lead to a court scrape and cause the men of the law to interfere with me.

"O Dear Mother, when any of my loved ones pass this place wherein he (she) lives, again slander reaches their tender ears so that there can be no peace in the neighborhood. When anyone comes to visit the place where I live, he (she) lies in wait for my guests to leave. Then harsh words of blasphemy and reproach reach my friend's ears.

"O Grand and Great Mother, can you not in your great wisdom tell me which evil spirits make this man (woman) so successful in his (her) magical work of the devil? All I desire is much new hope, to protect my home and my loved ones, and in the end to attain peace of mind and harmony. My Dear Mother, please hear my plea, my hopeful prayer. Please hasten to enlighten me so that all the things I have requested of thee shall soon come unto me your faithful servant. Allow all the things I wish, O Dear One, and I shall remain true to you forever. "I know, O Great One, it surely is the Spirit of Restlessness and the Spirit of Envy that wage this warfare and urge my neighbor to bother me. These same evil forces speak words through him (her) which cause trouble and dire problem; among my other good neighbors.

I beg of thee to placate these evil spirits with your all supreme might and power. I will, as you require, treat my neighbor in the spirit of peace and righteousness. My tongue shall be stilled of everything but kindness and my mind shall generate nothing but sweet and pure thoughts. I will do all of these things, O Great Mother, and win everything in the end. So be it."

TO PROTECT AGAINST IMPRISONMENT

Arrange the table or altar as illustrated in Chapter two. Light your two Monthly Vibratory Candles, two Daily Cross Candles, and the following Special Purpose Candles: one dark blue, one orchid, one white, and one purple. Close your eyes, concentrate, and then carefully repeat this invocation:

"O Grand Mother of All Things, O Mother of Spirits, I come unto you in this time of trial and tribulation. O Good Mother, I am sore of feet and heavy of heart. The power of evil men has directed that I shall be placed in the darkest of dungeons. I am told that I shall be deprived of the beauty, pleasures, and good will of the world. My former good friends now look down upon me and they show great displeasure with all that I say and do. They pass me with face turned away.

"O Mother Dear Mother, my enemies vilify me and say untruths, blasphemy, and perjuring statements. To my dismay, people point their fingers at me when they pass me on the streets of the city. They loudly condemn all those dear to me and those who love and trust me.

"O Great Mother, I say unto you that I shall come before the judges and the scribes and the law men. I plead for your kind intervention and assistance when these people pass judgment upon me. Aid me, O Mother of Spirits, according to my faith and my hope. Let me be fairly judged according to my sacrifice and invocations to you In the past and according to your wise counsel. But allow me to not be judged by the ever smooth tongues of the lying witnesses and the men of law.

"I promise, O Mother, that on the day the judges shall call upon me to come forth to trial, I shall obey them. I shall take with me my man of law and my witnesses. And with your great power over all things, the judge shall have to quietly listen to the testimony of my friends. I know, O Great Mother, that the judge will hear me and be fair. He shall believe in me and he shall deal with me with mildness."

To Remove Evil Influences

Arrange the table or altar as illustrated in Chapter two. Light your two Monthly Vibratory Candles, two Daily Cross Candles, and the following Special Purpose Candles: one orchid, one white, and one purple. Close your eyes, concentrate, and then carefully repeat this invocation:

"O My Mother of Love, I come unto you and say my house has been crossed and confusion reigns everywhere. Good Mother, where there should be peace, words of bitter regret are so often spoken in haste. Where there should be words of praise, words of doubt and jealousy are shouted about. Where there should be words of love, where only confidence and good will should be found, words of strife and crossed purposes are constantly bantered back and forth.

"O Good Mother, my dear ones look upon me with suspicion. Strangers hearken not unto my voice. Neither does anyone now believe my words even when I speak them with respect and truth. The stranger leaves my house in anger. My loved ones do not come around to comfort me. I am desolate, uncared for, unloved, and most miserable. I am sorely at a loss to overcome this terrible calamity which has befallen me.

"O My Good and Great Mother, I humbly pray for you to look with more favor on your broken-spirited child. I beg of you to help me through my troubled times, and to fill my house with nothing but good spirits. Please, O Mother Dear, give me cheer and comfort where there is now only strife and evil pressures. Make the stranger speak to me with

respect and with a sweeter voice. Make both the stranger and my loved ones and my friends believe in me once again. Make them all hearken to my words that I may have my way with them.

"I Promise, O Great Mother, to do all things better than I have tried to do in the past. When I meet my loved ones and my friends and my relatives at the door, I shall greet them all with a clear face and honest words. I will sympathize with all people I meet and they will surely bring me cheer. I know, with your blessed help O Mother, that the evil spirits shall be forever conquered. The evil spirits shall remain away from my place and only the good spirits shall remain."

8

Secret Spells for Drawing Love

To Increase the Passion of a Lover

Arrange the table or altar as illustrated in Chapter two. Light your two Montllly Vibratory Candles and your two Daily Cross Candles. Then carefully blend the following ingredients in a plain white dish:

Dragon's Blood Incense	*1/2 teaspoon*
Musk Incense	*1/2 teaspoon*
Black Cat Bone Incense	*1 teaspoon*
Love Desire Incense	*1 teaspoon*
Mixed Root Incense	*1/4 teaspoon*

When the above is thoroughly mixed, sprinkle the table or altar with a small amount of **Lover's Oil and Dominating Oil**. Then put the incense blend in your two incense burners on the table or altar and light. Sprinkle a small amount of **Spikenard Powder and Attraction Powder** on your naked body. Rub a little **Oriental Lovers Sachet** around your genital region. Now close your eyes and concentrate on your lover for a full seven minutes. When finished, rise and blow out the candles. Repeat this entire ritual for seven successive days at the exact same time.

Secret Spells for Drawing Love

To Sexually Control Someone With Sensuality

Arrange the table or altar as illustrated in Chapter two. Light your two Monthly Vibratory Candles and your two Daily Cross Candles. Then carefully blend the following ingredients in a plain white dish:

Luv, Luv, Luv Incense	1 teaspoon
Attraction Incense	1/2 teaspoon
Fire of Love Incense	1 teaspoon
Musk Incense	1/4 teaspoon
Eye of a Cat Incense	1/4 teaspoon

When the above is thoroughly mixed, sprinkle the table or altar with a small amount of **French Love Powder, Lovers Fire Powder, and Master's Powder**. Then put the incense blend in your two incense burners on the table or altar and light. Sprinkle a small amount of **Luv, Luv, Luv Oil and Lovers Fire Oil** on your naked body. Rub a little **French Love Sachet** around your genital region. Now close your eyes and concentrate on whom you desire to control for a full seven minutes. When finished, rise and blow out the candles. Repeat this entire ritual for seven successive days at the exact same time.

To Incite a Desired Lover to Passion

Arrange the table or altar as illustrated in Chapter two. Light your two Monthly Vibratory Candles and your two Daily Cross Candles. Then carefully blend the following ingredients in a plain white dish:

Musk Incense	1 teaspoon
7th Heaven Incense	1/4 teaspoon
Goona Goona Incense	1/4 teaspoon
Garden of Love Incense	1/2 teaspoon
Love Incense	1/2 teaspoon

When the above is thoroughly mixed, sprinkle the table or altar with a small amount of **Passion Flower Oil and Teasing Lover Oil**.

Then put the incense blend in your two incense burners on the table or altar and light. Sprinkle a small amount of *Orris Root Powder, Fire of Love Powder, and Honeysuckle Oil* on your naked body. Rub a little *Lovers Oil* around your genital region. Now close your eyes and concentrate on your lover's sex organ for a full seven minutes. When finished, rise and blow out all of the candles. Repeat this entire ritual for seven successive days at the exact same time.

To Gain More Than One Good Lover

Arrange the table or altar as illustrated in Chapter two. Light your two Monthly Vibratory Candles and your two Daily Cross Candles. Then carefully blend the following ingredients in a plain white dish:

Attraction for Love Incense	1 teaspoon
Passion Flower Incense	1/2 teaspoon
Love Incense	1/4 teaspoon
5 Finger Incense	1/4 teaspoon
High John the Conquerer Incense	1/2 teaspoon

When the above is thoroughly mixed, sprinkle the table or altar with a small amount of *Master of the Woods Powder and Queen's Root Powder*. Then put the incense m your two incense burners on the table or altar and light. Sprinkle a small amount of *Rue Oil and Adam and Eve Oil* on your naked body. Rub a little *Lovage Oil* around your genital region. Now close your eyes and concentrate on more than one lover in your arms for a full seven minutes. When finished, rise and blow out the candles. Repeat this entire ritual for seven successive days at the exact same time.

To Protect Against Being Hurt by a False Lover

Arrange the table or altar as illustrated in Chapter two. Light your two Monthly Vibratory Candles and your two Daily Cross Candles. Then carefully blend the following ingredients in a plain white dish:

Secret Spells for Drawing Love

Drive Away Roots Incense	1/2 teaspoon
Attraction for Love Incense	1/4 teaspoon
7 Devils Incense	1 teaspoon
Confusion Incense	1 teaspoon
Protection Incense	1/4 teaspoon

When the above is thoroughly blended, put the mixture in your two incense burners on the table or altar and light. Then rub your genital region with an equal mixture of **Red Rose Oil and Night of Love Oil**. Close your eyes and concentrate on the spell's purpose for a full seven minutes. Lastly, repeat the following benediction three times:

"Our dear Lord Jesus Christ going on a journey saw a firebrand burning. It was Saint Lorenzo stretched out on a roasting-spit. Our Lord Jesus rendered him assistance and consolation. Jesus lifted his divine hand and blessed the good saint. Jesus made the fire stop from spreading deeper and wider. Thus may the burning of heartbreak and unhappy love be blessed in the name of God the Father, God the Son, and God the Holy Ghost. Amen. Amen. Amen."

When finished, rub your body with a small amount of **John the Conqueror Oil and Holy Prophets Oil**. Then rise and blow out the candles. Repeat this entire ritual for seven consecutive days at the exact same time. Then just before going to bed, say the Lord's PrayeT three times.

To Improve the Quality of Lovemaking

Arrange the table or altar as illustrated in Chapter two. Light your two Monthly Vibratory Candles and your two Daily Cross Candles. Then carefully blend the following ingredients in a plain white dish:

Queen Elizabeth Root Incense	1 teaspoon
Cleopatra Incense	1/4 teaspoon
7 Holy Spirits Incense	1/2 teaspoon
Ancient Wisdom Incense	1/4 teaspoon
Love Incense	1 teaspoon
Goddess of Love Incense	1 teaspoon

When the above is thoroughly mixed, sprinkle the table or altar with a small amount of *Musk Lover's Oil and Spiritual Inspiration Oil.* Then put the incense blend in your two incense burners on the table or altar and light. Sprinkle a small amount of *Kindly Spirit Powder and Blessing of Allah Powder* on your naked body. Rub a little *Night Queen Oil* around your genital region. Now close your eyes and concentrate on various lovemaking techniques for a full seven minutes. When finished, rise and blow out the candles. Repeat this entire ritual for seven successive days at the exact same time.

To Stop a Lover From Becoming Jealous or Possessive

Arrange the table or altar as illustrated in Chapter two. Light your two Monthly Vibratory Candles and your two Daily Cross Candles. Then carefully blend the following ingredients in a plain white dish:

Protection Incense	1/4 teaspoon
Chaser Incense	1/4 teaspoon
Psychic Powers Incense	1 teaspoon
Magnolia Incense	1 teaspoon
Yerba Mate Incense	1 teaspoon

When the above is thoroughly mixed, sprinkle the table or altar with a small amount of *Gypsy Witch Oil and Heavenly Scent Oil.* Then put the incense blend in your two incense burners on the table or altar and light. Sprinkle a small amount of *Fire of Love Powder and Spanish Fire Powder* on your naked body. Rub a little *Stay at Home Oil* around your genital region. Now close your eyes and concentrate on your jealous lover or mate for a full seven minutes. When finished, rise and blow out the candles. Repeat this entire ritual for seven successive days at the exact same time.

SECRET SPELLS FOR DRAWING LOVE

TO TOTALLY GAIN CONTROL OVER A LOVER

Arrange the table or altar as illustrated in Chapter two. Light your two Monthly Vibratory Candles and your two Daily Cross Candles. Then carefully blend the following ingredients in a plain white dish:

Cassia Incense	*1/4 teaspoon*
Attraction Incense	*1 teaspoon*
Garden of Love Incense	*1/2 teaspoon*
Compelling Incense	*1 teaspoon*
Domination Incense	*1/4 teaspoon*
Irresistible Incense	*1 teaspoon*

When the above is thoroughly mixed, sprinkle the table or altar with a small amount of **Adam and Eve Oil and Red Rose Oil**. Then put the incense blend in your two incense burners on the table or altar and light. Sprinkle a small amount of **Rosemary Powder and Jezebel Root Powder** on your naked body. Rub a little **Jezebel Root Oil** around your genital region. Now close your eyes and concentrate on gaining control of a lover for a full seven minutes. When finished, rise and blow out the candles. Repeat this entire ritual for seven successive days at the exact same time.

A SPECIAL SPELL FOR ATTRACTING NEW LOVE

Arrange the table or altar as illustrated in Chapter two. Light your two Monthly Vibratory Candles and your two Daily Cross Candles. Then carefully blend the following ingredients in a plain white dish:

Lover's Incense	*1/2 teaspoon*
Love Drawing Incense	*1/4 teaspoon*
Come To Me Incense	*1 teaspoon*
Venus Incense	*1 teaspoon*
Goddess Aphrodite Incense	*1/2 teaspoon*

When the above is thoroughly blended, put the mixture in your two incense burners on the table or altar and light. Then close your eyes and concentrate on the spell's purpose for a full seven minutes. Lastly, repeat the following benediction three times:

"Jesus, I will arise. Jesus, do Thou accompany me? Jesus, do Thou lock my heart into Thine? And do Thou let my body and my soul be commended unto Thee? The Lord is crucified. May God guard my senses that evil spirits may not overcome me. May God grant me my dearest wish for someone to love and care for me. In the name of God the Father, God the Son, and God the Holy Ghost. Amen. Amen. Amen."

When finished, rub your body with a small amount of **John the Conqueror Oil and Holy Prophets Oil.** Then rise and blow out the candles. Repeat this entire ritual for seven consecutive days at the exact same time. Then. just before going to bed, say the Lord's Prayer three times.

9

Secret Spells for a Happy Marriage

To Force a Lover to Marry You

Arrange the table or altar as illustrated in Chapter two. Light your two Monthly Vibratory Candles and your two Daily Cross Candles. Then carefully blend the following ingredients in a plain white dish:

Loveage Root Incense	*1/4 teaspoon*
Buckeye Incense	*1/4 teaspoon*
Fire of Love Incense	*1 teaspoon*
Kyphi Incense	*1/4 teaspoon*
St. Mary Incense	*1 teaspoon*

When the above is thoroughly mixed, sprinkle the table or altar with a small amount of **Beneficial Powder** and **Gardenia Powder**. Then put the incense blend in your two incense burners on the table or altar and light. Sprinkle a small amount of **Goldstone Oil and Teasing Lover Oil** on your naked body. Now close your eyes and concentrate on your lover's genitals for a full seven minutes. When finished, rise and blow out the candles. Repeat this entire ritual for seven successive days at the exact same time.

To Aid in Your Marriage Prospects

Arrange the table or altar as illustrated in Chapter two. Light your two Monthly Vibratory Candles and your two Daily Cross Candles. Then carefully blend the following ingredients in a plain white dish:

Waahoo Bark Incense	*1 teaspoon*
Coconut Incense	*1/4 teaspoon*
4 Leaf Clover Incense	*1/4 teaspoon*
Love Incense	*1/2 teaspoon*
Solomon's Incense	*1/4 teaspoon*
Marriage Incense	*1 teaspoon*

When the above is thoroughly mixed, sprinkle the table or altar with a small amount of **Attraction Oil and Lodestone Oil.** Then put the incense blend in your two incense burners on the table or altar and light. Sprinkle a small amount of **Adam and Eve Powder and Red Rose Powder** on your naked body. Now close your eyes and concentrate on getting married for a full seven minutes. When finished, rise and blow out the candles. Repeat this entire ritual for seven successive days at the exact same time.

To Bring More Lovemaking to Your Marriage Bed

Arrange the table or altar as illustrated in Chapter two. Light your two Monthly Vibratory Candles and your two Daily Cross Candles. Then carefully blend the following ingredients in a plain white dish:

Passion Flower Incense	*1 teaspoon*
7 Circles Incense	*1/4 teaspoon*
Abracadabra Incense	*1/4 teaspoon*
Crown of Success Incense	*1/4 teaspoon*
Hand of Glory Incense	*1/4 teaspoon*

Secret Spells for a Happy Marriage

When the above is thoroughly mixed, sprinkle the table or altar with a small amount of ***Queen's Root Oil and Lover's Oil.*** Then put the incense blend in your two lincense burners on the table or altar and light. Sprinkle a small amount of ***Good Life Powder and Loving Herb Powder*** on your naked body. Rub some ***Fire of Love Oil*** on your genitals. Now close your eyes and concentrate on your marriage mate for a full seven minutes. Repeat this entire ritual for seven successive days at the exact same time.

To Force Your Partner to Stay Faithful

Arrange the table or altar as illustrated in Chapter two. Light your two Monthly Vibratory Candles and your two Daily Cross Candles. Then carefully blend the following ingredients in a plain white dish:

Laurel Leaves Incense	1 teaspoon
Power Incense	1/4 teaspoon
Horseshoe Incense	1/4 teaspoon
Flaming Power Incense	1/2 teaspoon
Occult Masters Incense	1 teaspoon

When the above is thoroughly mixed, sprinkle the table or altar with a small amount of ***Seven Barks Powder and Passion Flower Powder.*** Then put the incense blend in your two incense burners on the table or altar and light. Sprinkle a small amount of ***Adam and Eve Oil and Heart Ease Oil*** on your naked body. Now close your eyes and concentrate on your mate's genitals for a full seven minutes. When finished, rise and blow out the candles. Repeat this entire ritual for seven consecutive days at the exact same time.

To Find the Perfect Marriage Mate

Arrange the table or altar as illustrated in Chapter two. Light your two Monthly Vibratory Candles and your two Daily Cross Candles. Then carefully blend the following ingredients in a plain white dish:

Love Desire Incense	1 teaspoon
Attracion Incense	1/2 teaspoon
Dreams Incense	1/2 teaspoon
Fiery Command Incense	1 teaspoon

When the above is thoroughly blended, put the mixture in your two incense burners on the table or altar and light. Then close your eyes and concentrate on finding a perfect marriage mate for a full seven minutes. Lastly, repeat the following benediction three times:

> *"There are three lilies standing upon the grave of the Lord our God. The first one is for the courage of God. The second represents the blood of Jesus. And the third one stands for the will of God. Stand still, lover! No more than Jesus Christ stepped down from His cross, no more shalt thou move from this spot! This I command thee by the four evangelists and elements of heaven, there in the river, or in the judgment, or in the sight. Thus I conjure thee by the last judgment to stand still and not move, until I see all the stars in heaven and the sun rises again. Thus I stop running and jumping and searching for my love. I command it all in the name of Jesus. Amen. Amen. Amen."*

When finished, rise and blow out the candles. Repeat this entire ritual for seven consecutive days at the exact same time. Then, just before going to bed, say the Lord's Prayer three times.

To Force a Wandering Mate to Return

Arrange the table or altar as illustrated in Chapter two. Light your two Monthly Vibratory Candles and your two Daily Cross Candles. Then carefully blend the following ingredients in a plain white dish:

Mistletoe Herb Incense	1/2 teaspoon
Spanish Fire Incense	1/4 teaspoon
Compelling Incense	1 teaspoon
Horn of Plenty Incense	1/4 teaspoon
Draw Back Incense	1/4 teaspoon
St. Michael Incense	1/4 teaspoon

SECRET SPELLS FOR A HAPPY MARRIAGE

When the above is thoroughly mixed, sprinkle the table or altar with a small amount of **Secrets of Love Powder and Oriental Lovers Powder**. Then put the incense blend in your two incense burners on the table or altar and light. Sprinkle a small amount of **Compelling Oil and Lady Luck Oil** on your naked body. Now close your eyes and concentrate on your wandering mate for a full seven minutes. When finished, rise and blow out the candles Repeat this entire ritual for seven successive days at the exact same time.

To Dream Who Your Future Mate Will Be

Arrange the table or altar as illustrated in Chapter two. Light your two Monthly Vibratory Candles and your two Daily Cross Candles, then carefully blend the following ingredients in a plain white dish:

Heart Ease Incense	1/4 teaspoon
Gold Lotus Temple Incense	1/2 teaspoon
Dove's Blood Incense	1/4 teaspoon
Happy Dreams Incense	1/2 teaspoon
Lavender Incense	1/2 teaspoon

When the above is thoroughly mixed, sprinkle the table or altar with a small amount of **Cassia Powder and Loving Herbs Powder.** Then put the incense blend in your two incense burners on the table or altar and light. Sprinkle a small amount of *Jezebel Root Oil and Attraction Oil* on your naked body. Now close your eyes and concentrate on dreaming of your future wedded bliss for a full seven minutes. When finished, rise and blow out the candles. Repeat this entire ritual for seven successive days at the exact same time.

To Bring Forth a Proposal of Marriage

Arrange the table or altar as illustrated in Chapter two. Light your two Monthly Vibratory Candles and your two Daily Cross Candles. Then carefully blend the following ingredients in a plain white dish:

Balsam Incense	1/4 teaspoon
Confusion Incense	1/4 teaspoon
Lover's Incense	1 teaspoon
Fiery Command Incense	1/2 teaspoon
Garden of Love Incense	1 teaspoon

When the above is thoroughly mixed, sprinkle the table or altar with a small amount of **Merciful Heaven Powder and Love Desire Powder.** Then put the incense blend in your two incense burners on the table or altar and light. Sprinkle a small amount of **Hand of Glory Oil and Cupid Drops Oil** on your naked body. Now close your eyes and concentrate on the person you wish to get a marriage proposal from for a full seven minutes. When finished, rise and blow out the candles. Repeat this entire ritual for seven successive days at the exact same time.

To Discover a Suitable Mate Among Your Friends

Arrange the table or altar as illustrated in Chapter two. Light your two Monthly Vibratory Candles and your two Daily Cross Candles. Then carefully blend the following ingredients in a plain white dish:

Grains of Paradise Incense	1/2 teaspoon
Lady Luck Incense	1/4 teaspoon
Blessing of Allah Incense	1/2 teaspoon
Musk Incense	1/4 teaspoon
Fiery Command Incense	1 teaspoon

When the above is thoroughly mixed, sprinkle the table or altar with a small amount of **Flaming Power Oil** and **Cleopatt a Oil.** Then put the incense blend in your two incense burners on the table or altar and light. Sprinkle a small amount of *Blessing Powder* and *Narcissus Powder* on your naked body. Rub a little *White Rose Oil* on your inner thighs. Now close your eyes and concentrate on finding a suitable mate among those you are friendly with. Do this for a full seven minutes. When finished, rise and blow out the candles. Repeat this entire ritual for seven successive days at the exact same time.

TO STOP A WAYWARD MATE FROM SEEING A LOVER

Arrange the table or altar as illustrated in Chapter two. Light your two Monthly Vibratory Candles and your two Daily Cross Candles. Then carefully blend the following ingredients in a plain white dish:

Fire of Love Incense	1 teaspoon
Glow of Attraction Incense	1/2 teaspoon
Flaming Power Incense	1/2 teaspoon

When the above is thoroughly blended, put the mixture in your two incense burners on the table or altar and light. Then close your eyes and concentrate on your wayward mate for a full seven minutes. Lastly, repeat the following benediction three times:

"Clear out, brand, but never in; be thou cold or hot, thou must cease to burn for someone else. May God guard thy blood and thy flesh, thy marrow and thy bones, and every artery, great and small. They all shall be guarded and protected in the name of God against inflammation of a false love. In the name of God, the Father, the Son, and the Holy Ghost. Amen. Amen. Amen."

When finished, rise and blow out the candles. Repeat this entire ritual for seven consecutive days at the exact same time. Then, just before going to bed, say the Lord's Prayer three times.

10

SECRET SPELLS FOR DRAWING GOOD FORTUNE

TO OVERCOME ADVERSITY

Arrange the table or altar as illustrated in Chapter two. Light your two Monthly Vibratory Candles and your two Daily Cross Candles. Then carefully blend the following ingredients in a plain white dish:

Rosemary Incense	1/4 teaspoon
Money Incense	1/4 teaspoon
Caridad Del Cobre Incense	1 teaspoon
Prosperity Incense	1 teaspoon
High Conquering Incense	1/2 teaspoon

When the above is thoroughly mixed, sprinkle the table or altar with a small amount of **Kindly Spirit Oil and Lady Luck Oil.** Then pu t the incense blend in your two incense burners on the table or al tar and light. Sprinkle a small amount of **Glow of Attraction Powder, Horseshoe Powder, and Holiness Trinity Powder** on your naked body. Now close your eyes and concentrate on your problem for a full seven minutes. When finished, rise and blow out the candles. Repeat this entire ritual for seven successive days at the exact same time.

SECRET SPELLS FOR DRAWING GOOD FORTUNE

TO ATTRACT LUCKIER VIBRATIONS IN YOUR LIFE

Arrange the table or altar as illustrated in Chapter two. Light your two Monthly Vibratory Candles and your two Daily Cross Candles. Then carefully blend the following ingredients in a plain white dish:

Planet Incense	*1/4 teaspoon*
Lucky Hand Incense	*1/2 teaspoon*
Jockey Club Incense	*1/4 teaspoon*
Kindly Spirit Incense	*1 teaspoon*
4-Leaf Clover Incense	*1 teaspoon*

When the above is thoroughly mixed, sprinkle the table or altar with a small amount of **4-Leaf Clover Powder and Money Powder**. Then put the incense blend in your two incense burners on the table or altar and light. Sprinkle a small amount of **Holy Prophet Oil and Conquering Glory Oil** on your naked body. Now close your eyes and concentrate on your desire for better luck for a full seven minutes. When finished, rise and blow out the candles. Repeat this entire ritual for seven successive days at the exact same time.

TO OVERWHELM ALL BAD LUCK

Arrange the table or altar as illustrated in Chapter two. Light your two Monthly Vibratory Candles and your two Daily Cross Candles. Then carefully blend the following ingredients in a plain white dish:

Lucky Hand Incense	*1/2 teaspoon*
Drawing Incense	*1/4 teaspoon*
Exodus Incense	*1/4 teaspoon*
Wishing Incense	*1/4 teaspoon*
Queen of the Night Incense	*1/2 teaspoon*
Occult Ceremony Incense	*1 teaspoon*

When the above is thoroughly mixed, sprinkle the table or altar with a small amount of *Uncrossing Powder and Olibanum Powder.* Then put the incense blend in your two incense burners on the table or altar and light. Sprinkle a small amount of *Magnet Oil and Lady Luck Oil* on your naked body. Now close your eyes and concentrate on overcoming the bad luck which has befallen you for a full seven minutes. When finished, rise and blow out the candles. Repeat this entire ritual for seven successive days at the exact same time.

To Make Better Things Happen in Your Life

Arrange the table or altar as illustrated in Chapter two. Light your two Monthly Vibratory Candles and your two Daily Cross Candles. Then carefully blend the following ingredients in a plain white dish:

Lucky Dog Incense	*1/2 teaspoon*
Midnight Ritual Incense	*1/4 teaspoon*
Come To Me Incense	*1 teaspoon*
Eye of the Cat Incense	*1/4 teaspoon*
Easy Life Incense	*1/2 teaspoon*

When the above is thoroughly mixed, sprinkle the table or altar with a small amount of *Seven Sisters Oil and Dominating Oil.* Then put the incense blend in your two incense burners on the table or altar and light. Sprinkle a small amount of *Come To Me Powder, Wealthy Way Powder, and Lucky Lodestone Powder* on your naked body. Now close your eyes and concentrate on happiness for a full seven minutes. When finished, rise and blow out the candles. Repeat this entire ritual for seven successive days at the exact same time.

To Attract Much Better Luck and Fortune

Arrange the table or altar as illustrated in Chapter two. Light your two Monthly Vibratory Candles and your two Daily Cross Candles. Then carefully blend the following ingredients in a plain white dish:

Lucky Hand Incense	*1 teaspoon*
Lady Luck Incense	*1/2 teaspoon*
Good Life Incense	*1/2 teaspoon*

When the above is thoroughly blended, put the mixture in your two incense burners on the table or altar and light. Then close your eyes and concentrate on happy things for a full seven minutes. Lastly, repeat the following benediction three times:

"Our Lord Jesus Christ stepped into the hall, and the Jews searched for Him everywhere. Thus shalt those who now speak evil of me with their false tongues, and contend against me, one day bear sorrows, be silenced, dumbstruck, intimidated, and abused, forever and ever, through the glory of God. The glory of God shall assist me in gaining good fortune and to avoid bad fortune. Do thou aid me forever and ever. Amen. Amen. Amen. Amen. Amen."

When finished, rise and blow out the candles. Repeat this entire ritual for seven consecutive days at the exact same time. Then, just before going to bed, say the Lord's Prayer three times.

To Help Bring Good Fortune to Your Life

Arrange the table or altar as illustrated in Chapter two. Light your two Monthly Vibratory Candles and your two Daily Cross Candles. Then carefully blend the following ingredients in a plain white dish:

Hi-Altar Incense	1 teaspoon
Goldstone Incense	1/4 teaspoon
Horn of Plenty Incense	1/2 teaspoon
Kabala Number Incense	1/4 teaspoon
Glow of Attraction Incense	1/2 teaspoon

When the above is thoroughly mixed, sprinkle the table or altar with a small amount of **Psalm Oil, Crown of Success Oil, and Arabian Nights Oil.** Then put the incense blend in your two incense burners on the table or altar and light. Sprinkle a small amount of **Lucky Hand Powder and Hand of Glory Powder** on your naked body. Now close your eyes and concentrate on what you desire most in your life for a full seven minutes. When finished, rise and blow out the candles. Repeat this entire ritual for seven consecutive days at the exact same time.

TO IMPROVE YOUR LIFE'S POSITION AND STATUS

Arrange the table or altar as illustrated in Chapter two. Light your two Monthly Vibratory Candles and your two Daily Cross Candles. Then carefully blend the following ingredients in a plain white dish:

7 Circle Incense	1/2 teaspoon
7th Heaven Incense	1/4 teaspoon
Power Incense	1/4 teaspoon
Conquering Glory Incense	1/4 teaspoon
Get Away Incense	1/4 teaspoon
Lost and Away Incense	1/4 teaspoon
Hot Foot Incense	1/2 teaspoon

When the above is thoroughly mixed, sprinkle the table or altar with a small amount of **Blessing of Allah Oil and Gospel Oil.** Then put the incense blend in your two incense burners on the table or altar and light. Sprinkle a small amount of **Good Life Powder and All Saints Powder** on your naked body. Now close your eyes and concentrate on what you desire most out of life for seven full minutes. When finished, rise and blow out the candles. Repeat this entire ritual for seven successive days at the exact same time.

11

Secret Spells for Financial Gain

To Attract Lots of Money

Arrange the table or altar as illustrated in Chapter two. Light your two Monthly Vibratory Candles and your two Daily Cross Candles. Then carefully blend the following ingredients in a plain white dish:

Wealthy Way Incense	1 teaspoon
Lucky Lodestone Incense	1/4 teaspoon
Fast Luck Incense	1/4 teaspoon
Glow of Attraction Incense	1/2 teaspoon
Jupiter Incense	1/2 teaspoon

When the above is thoroughly mixed, sprinkle the table or altar with a small amount of **Lucky Dog Oil and Master's Oil.** Then put the incense blend in your two incense burners on the table or altar and light. Sprinkle asmall amount of **Nettle Nutmeg Powder and Black Snake Root Powder** on your naked body. Now close your eyesand concentrate on how much money you want for a full seven minutes. When finished, rise and blow out the candles. Repeat this entire ritual for seven successive days at the exact same time.

To Better Succeed and Make Money

Arrange the table or altar as illustrated in Chapter two. Light your two Monthly Vibratory Candles and your two Daily Cross Candles. Then carefully blend the following ingredients in a plain white dish:

Come To Me Incense	*1 teaspoon*
Golden Orient Incense	*1/4 teaspoon*
Money Incense	*1 teaspoon*
Flaming Power Incense	*1/4 teaspoon*
Has No Hanna Incense	*1/4 teaspoon*
Mecca Incense	*1/4 teaspoon*

When the above is thoroughly mixed, sprinkle the table or altar with a small amount of **Irish Moss Powder, Sour Grass Powder, and Lucky Hand Root Powder**. Then put the incense blend in your two incense burners on the table or altar and light. Sprinkle a small amount of **Money Drawing Oil, Angel's Oil, and Compelling Oil** on your naked body. Now close your eyes and concentrate on success and money for a full seven minutes. When finished, rise and blow out the candles. Repeat this entire ritual for seven successive days at the exact same time.

To Obtain a Raise on the Job

Arrange the table or altar as illustrated in Chapter two. Light your two Monthly Vibratory Candles and your two Daily Cross Candles. Then carefully blend the following ingredients in a plain white dish:

Lucky Incense	*1 teaspoon*
Angel's Delight Incense	*1/2 teaspoon*
Money Attraction Incense	*1 teaspoon*
Invocation Incense	*1/4 teaspoon*
Success Incense	*1/2 teaspoon*

When the above is thoroughly mixed, sprinkle the table or altar with a small amount of **High Power Oil and Indian Guide Oil.**

Then put the incense blend in your two incense burners on the table or altar and light. Sprinkle a small amount of *Hound's Tongue Powder, Burning Bush Powder, and Sweet Rush Powder* on your naked body. Now close your eyes and concentrate on your desired raise or job advancement for a full seven minutes. When finished, rise and blow out the candles. Repeat this entire ritual for seven successive days at the exact same time.

TO BRING MORE MONEY AND SUCCESS IN EVERYTHING

Arrange the table or altar as illustrated in Chapter two. Light your two Monthly Vibratory Candles and your two Daily Cross Candles. Then carefully blend the following ingredients in a plain white dish:

Money Drawing Incense	*1 teaspoon*
Horn of Plenty Incense	*1/2 teaspoon*
Draw Back Incense	*1/2 teaspoon*

When the above is thoroughly blended, put the mixture in your two incense burners on the table or altar and light. Then close your eyes and concentrate on the spell's purpose for a full seven minutes. Lastly; repeat the following benediction three times:

"Christ's cross and Christ's crown, Christ Jesus' colored blood, be thou every hour good. God, the Father, is beside me. God, the Son, is before me. God, the Holy Ghost, is behind me. Nothing can possibly go wrong in my life. Money come. Money come. Success come. Success come. Amen. Amen."

When finished, rub your body with a small amount of *John the Conqueror Oil and Holy Prophets Oil*. Then rise and blow out the candles. Repeat this entire ritual for seven consecutive days at the exact same time. Then, just before going to bed; say the Lord's Prayer three times.

To Overcome Financial Reverses

Arrange the table or altar as illustrated in Chapter two. Light your two Monthly Vibratory Candles and your two Daily Cross Candles. Then carefully blend the following ingredients in a plain white dish:

Brahma Incense	*1/4 teaspoon*
Lady Luck Incense	*1/2 teaspoon*
Deliverance Incense	*1 teaspoon*
Go Away Evil Incense	*1/2 teaspoon*
Conquering Glory Incense	*1/4 teaspoon*

When the above is thoroughly mixed, sprinkle the table or altar with a small amount of **Freedom Oil, Spiritual Inspiration Oil, and Gypsy Player's Hand Oil**. Then put the incense blend in your two incense burners on the table or altar and light. Sprinkle a small amount of **Lodestone Powder** and **Bluebird of Happiness Powder** on your naked body. Now close your eyes and concentrate on your financial problem for a full seven minutes. When finished, rise and blow out the candles. Repeat this entire ritual for seven successive days at the exact same time.

To Receive a Financial Blessing Where in Need

Arrange the table or altar as illustrated in Chapter two. Light your two Monthly Vibratory Candles and your two Daily Cross Candles. Then carefully blend the following ingredients in a plain white dish:

5 Circle Incense	*1 teaspoon*
Mummy Incense	*1/4 teaspoon*
Zodiac Incense	*1/4 teaspoon*
3 Kings Incense	*1 teaspoon*
Money Blessing Incense	*1 teaspoon*

When the above is thoroughly mixed, sprinkle the table or altar with a small amount of *Success Oil, Attraction Oil, and Lucky Planet Oil.* Then put the incense blend in your two incense burners on the table or altar and light. Sprinkle a small amount of ***Dog Rose Powder and Kava Kava Powder*** on your naked body. Now close your eyes and concentrate on how much money you need for a full seven minutes. When finished, rise and blow out the candles. Repeat this entire ritual for seven successive days at the exact same time.

To Make Your Financial Prospects Much Better

Arrange the table or altar as illustrated in Chapter two. Light your two Monthly Vibratory Candles and your two Daily Cross Candles. Then carefully blend the following ingredients in a plain white dish:

Fast Luck Incense	*1/2 teaspoon*
John the Conqueror Incense	*1/2 teaspoon*
Wealthy Way Incense	*1/2 teaspoon*
Holy Prophet Incense	*1/4 teaspoon*
Crown of Success Incense	*1/4 teaspoon*
Business Incense	*1/4 teaspoon*
Overpower All Incense	*1/4 teaspoon*

When the above is thoroughly mixed, sprinkle the table or altar with a small amount of ***Jockey Club Powder and Mount Sinai Powder.*** Then put the incense blend in your two incense burners on the table or altar and light Sprinkle a small amount of ***King David Oil, Horn of Plenty Oil, and Merciful Heaven Oil*** on your naked body. Now close your eyes and concentrate on bettering your financial prospects for a full seven minutes. When finished, rise and blow out the candles. Repeat this entire ritual for seven successive days at the exact same time.

12

Secret Spells for Protection from Harm

To Avoid any Legal Trouble

Arrange the table or altar as illustrated in Chapter two. Light your two Monthly Vibratory Candles and your two Daily Cross Candles. Then carefully blend the following ingredients in a plain white dish:

Ground Eucalyptus Leaves	1/4 teaspoon
Fiery Wall of Protection Incense	1 teaspoon
10 Commandments Incense	1/4 teaspoon
Confusion Incense	1/4 teaspoon
Crown of Success Incense	1/4 teaspoon
Conquering Glory Incense	1/4 teaspoon

When the above is thoroughly mixed, sprinkle the table or altar with a small amount of **Spikenard Powder, Holy Powder, and Protection Powder**. Then put the incense blend in your two incense burners on the table or altar and light. Sprinkle a small amount of **Healing Oil and Seven Sisters Oil** on your naked body. Now close your eyes and concentrate on your legal complications for a full seven minutes. When finished, rise and blow out the candles. Repeat this entire ritual for seven successive days at the exact same time.

To Influence Someone Who Hates You

Arrange the table or altar as illustrated in Chapter two. Light your two Monthly Vibratory Candles and your two Daily Cross Candles. Then carefully blend the following ingredients in a plain white dish:

Black Musk Incense	*1/2 teaspoon*
Ground Thyme Leaves	*1/4 teaspoon*
Controlling Inccnse	*1 teaspoon*
Peaceful Home Incense	*1/2 teaspoon*
Spiritualist Incense	*1/4 teaspoon*

When the above is thoroughly mixed, sprinkle the table or altar with a small amount of ***Spirit Oil and King Solomon Oil***. Then put the incense blend in your two incense burners on the table or altar and light. Sprinkle a small amount of ***Cassia Powder, Fast Luck Powder, and Dominating Powder*** on your naked body. Now close your eyes and concentrate on the person who so detests you for a full seven minutes. When finished, rise and blow out the candles. Repeat this entire ritual for seven successive days at the exact same time.

To Remove all Obstacles from Your Path

Arrange the table or altar as illustrated in Chapter two. Light your two Monthly Vibratory Candles and your two Daily Cross Candles. Then carefully blend the following ingredients in a plain white dish:

Yerbamate Powder	*1/4 teaspoon*
Saffron Incense	*1/2 teaspoon*
Benzoin Incense	*1/4 teaspoon*
Cedar Wood Incense	*1/2 teaspoon*
Snake Root Incense	*1/2 teaspoon*
Lucky Rites Incense	*1 teaspoon*

When the above is thoroughly mixed, sprinkle the table or altar with a small amount of ***Four Thieves Vinegar*** and ***Ju Ju Oil.***

Then put the incense blend in your two incense burners on the table or altar and light. Sprinkle a small amount of *Asafoetida Powder and Peace Powder* on your naked body. Now close your eyes and concentrate on the obstacle for seven full minutes. When finished, rise and blow out the candles. Repeat this entire ritual for seven successive days at the exact same time.

To Change An Enemy's Mind

Arrange the table or altar as illustrated in Chapter two. Light your two Monthly Vibratory Candles and your two Daily Cross Candles. Then carefully blend the following ingredients in a plain white dish:

Five Finger Grass	1 piece
Chinese Powder Incense	1/2 teaspoon
Temple Snake Joss Incense	1/4 teaspoon
Jinx Incense	1/4 teaspoon
Lucky Hand Incense	1/2 teaspoon
Red Rose Oil Incense	1/4 teaspoon
Virjen del Carmen Incense	1/4 teaspoon

When the above is thoroughly mixed, sprinkle the table or altar with a small amount of *Van Van Perfume Oil* and *Bible Bouquet Oil.* Then put the incense blend in your two incense burners on the table or altar and light. Sprinkle a small amount of *Bible Bouquet Powder* and *Compelling Powder* on your naked body. Now close your eyes and concentrate on the enemy you wish to help. Continue this for seven full minutes. When finished, rise and blow out the candles. Repeat this entire ritual for seven successive days at the exact same time.

To Stop A Thief Before He Steals From You

Arrange the table or altar as illustrated in Chapter two. Light your two Monthly Vibratory Candles and your two Daily Cross Candles. Then carefully blend the following ingredients in a plain white dish:

Secret Spells for Protection from Harm

> Kindly Spirit Incense   1 teaspoon
> Banishing Incense   1 teaspoon
> Goofer Dust Incense   1/2 teaspoon

When the above is thoroughly blended, put the mixture in your two incense burners on the table or altar and light. Then close your eyes and concentrate on the spell's purpose for a full seven minutes. Lastly, repeat the following benediction three times:

> *"Thus shall rule it, God the Father, the Son, and the Holy Ghost. Amen. Thirty-three angels speak to each other coming to administer in company with Mary. Then spoke dear Daniel, the holy one: Trust not, my dear woman, I see some thieves coming who intend stealing your dear babe; this I cannot conceal from you. Then spake our dear Lady to Saint Peter: I have bound with a band, through Christ's hand; therefore, my thieves are bound even by the hand of Christ, if they wish to steal mine own, in the house, in the chest, upon the meadow or the fields, in the woods, in the orchard, in the vineyard, or in the garden, or wherever they intend to steal. Our dear Lady said: Whoever chooses may steal; yet if anyone does steal, he shall stand like a buck, he shall stand like a stake, and he shall count all the stones upon the earth and all the stars in the heavens. Thus I give thee leave, and command every spirit to be master over every thief, by the guardianship of Saint Daniel, and by the burden of this world's goods. And the countenance shall be unto thee, that thou canst not move from the spot, as long as my tongue in the flesh shall not give thee leave. This I command thee by the Holy Virgin Mary, the Mother of Jesus, by the power and might by which God has created heaven and earth, by the host of all the angels, and by the saints of God the Father, the Son, and he Holy Ghost. Amen."*

When finished, rise and blow out the candles. Repeat this entire ritual for seven consecutive days at the exact same time. Then, just before going to bed, say this benediction in little more than a whisper:

> *"Ye thieves, I conjure you, to be obedient like Jesus Christ, who obeyed His Heavenly Father*

unto the cross, and to stand without moving out of my sight, in the name of the Trinity. I command you by the power of God and the incarnation of Jesus Christ, not to move out of my sight, like Jesus Christ was standing on Jordan's stormy banks to be baptized by John. And furthermore, I conjure you to stand still and not to move out of my sight, like Jesus Christ did stand when He was about to be nailed to the cross to release the fathers of the church from the bonds of hell. Ye thieves, I bind you with the same bonds with which Jesus our Lord has bound hell; and thus ye shall be bound; and the same words that bind you shall also release you."

TO RESTRAIN SOMEONE WHO IS CAUSING DISTRESS

Arrange the table or altar as illustrated in Chapter two. Light your two Monthly Vibratory Candles and your two Daily Cross Candles. Then carefully blend the following ingredients in a plain white dish:

Ju Ju Oil	*1 drop*
John the Conqueror Incense	*1 teaspoon*
Crossing Incense	*1/4 teaspoon*
Orris Powder	*1/2 teaspoon*
Sandalwood Incense	*1/2 teaspoon*

When the above is thoroughly mixed, sprinkle the table or altar with a small amount of ***Obeah Oil and War Water***. Then put the incense blend in your two incense burners on the table or altar and light. Sprinkle a small amount of ***Success Oil and Balsam Oil*** on your naked body. Now close your eyes and concentrate on the person causing the problem for a full seven minutes. When finished, rise and blow out the candles. Repeat this entire ritual for seven successive days at the exact same time.

SECRET SPELLS FOR PROTECTION FROM HARM

TO DRIVE INSANITY AWAY FROM YOU AND INTO SOMEONE ELSE

Arrange the table or altar as illustrated in Chapter two. Light your two Monthly Vibratory Candles and your two Daily Cross Candles. Then carefully blend the following ingredients in a plain white dish:

Confusion Incense	1/2 teaspoon
Dominating Incense	1/4 teaspoon
Crossing Incense	1/4 teaspoon
Van Van Incense	1/4 teaspoon
Compelling Incense	1/4 teaspoon
Spirit Force Incense	1/2 teaspoon

When the above is thoroughly mixed, sprinkle the table or altar with a small amount of **Angels Oil and Lucky Planet Oil**. Then put the incense blend in your two incense burners on the table or altar and light. Sprinkle a small amount of **Uncrossing Powder, Jinx Removing Powder, and Master Power Powder** on your naked body. Now close your eyes and concentrate on the mental problem at hand for a full seven minutes. When finished, rise and blow out the candles. Repeat this entire ritual for seven successive days at the exact same time.

A POWERFUL SPELL TO OVERCOME ALL PROBLEMS

Arrange the table or altar as illustrated in Chapter two. Light your two Monthly Vibratory Candles and your two Daily Cross Candles. Then carefully blend the following ingredients in a plain white dish:

Orris Root Powder	1/4 teaspoon
Vanillan Incense	1/4 teaspoon
Ground Calendula Flowers	1/4 teaspoon
Peace Incense	1/2 teaspoon
Lucky Nine Mixture Incense	1/2 teaspoon

When the above is thoroughly mixed, sprinkle the table or altar with a small amount of *Graveyard Dust and Poke Root Powder.* Then put the incense blend in your two incense burners on the table or altar and light. Sprinkle a small amount of *Peace Oil and Lavendar Oil* on your naked body. Now close your eyes and concentrate on the problem at hand for a full seven minutes. When finished, rise and blow out the candles. Repeat this entire ritual for seven successive days at the exact same time.

To Overcome Disfavor

Arrange the table or altar as illustrated in Chapter two Light your two Monthly Vibratory Candles and your two Daily Cross Candles. Then carefully blend the following ingredients in a plain white dish:

Power Incense	*1/2 teaspoon*
Salt Peter	*1/8 teaspoon*
Conquering Incense	*1/4 teaspoon*
Musk Love Oil Incense	*1/4 teaspoon*
Hi-Altar Incense	*1/8 teaspoon*
Moses Incense	*1/2 teaspoon*
High Conqueror Incense	*1/2 teaspoon*
Conquering Glory Incense	*1/2 teaspoon*

When the above is thoroughly mixed, sprinkle the table or altar with a small amount of *Violet Powder and Compelling Powder.* Then put the incense blend in your two incense burners on the table or altar and light. Sprinkle a small amount of *Dove's Blood Oil, Buddha Oil, and Exodus Oil* on your naked body. Now close your eyes and concentrate on your problem for a full seven minutes. When finished, rise and blow out the candles. Repeat this entire ritual for seven consecutive days at the exact same time.

Secret Spells for Protection from Harm

To Compel a Thief to Return Stolen Goods

Arrange the table or altar as illustrated in Chapter two. Light your two Monthly Vibratory Candles and your two Daily Cross Candles. Then carefully blend the following ingredients in a plain white dish:

XX Double Cross Incense	*1 teaspoon*
Jinxing Incense	*1/2 teaspoon*
Flying Devil Incense	*1/2 teaspoon*
Babel Incense	*1/2 teaspoon*
Crossing Incense	*1/4 teaspoon*
Holy Cross Incense	*1/4 teaspoon*

When the above is thoroughly mixed, put the blend in your two incense burners on the table or altar and light. Rub your body down with a mixture of equal parts ***Invocation Oil and Occult Ceremony Oil***. Then take three nails from a used coffin, or three horseshoe nails that were never used. Hold these nails out toward the flickering candles and repeat the following benediction three times:

"O thief, I bind you by the first nail, which I drive in to thy skull and thy brain, to return the goods thou hast stolen to their former place. Thou shalt feel as sick and as anxious to see men, and to see the place you stole from, as felt the disciple Judas after betraying Jesus Christ. I bind thee by the second nail, which I drive into your lungs and liver, to return the stolen goods to their former place. Thou shalt feel as sick and as anxious to see men, and to see the place you have stolen from, as did Pilate in the fires of hell. The third nail I shall drive into thy foot, O thief, in order that thou shalt return the stolen goods to the very same place from which thou hast stolen them. O. thief, I bind thee and compel thee, by these three holy nails which were driven through the hands and the feet of Jesus Christ, to return the stolen goods to the very same place from which thou hast stolen them. Amen. Amen. Amen."

When finished, rise and blow out the candles. Early the next morning, before sunrise, take the same three nails and go stand under a young tree. Hold these three nails toward the rising sun and again repeat the above benediction. Return to your home, wrap the nails in clean black cotton cloth, and hide them in the corner of a dark closet. No one must be able to accidently stumble across the nails. Then recite the Lord's Prayer three times.

13

Secret Spells Against Illness & Death

To Overcome Any Kind of Illness

Arrange the table or altar as illustrated in Chapter two. Light your two Monthly Vibratory Candles and your two Daily Cross Candles. Then carefully blend the following ingredients in a plain white dish:

Moses Incense	1/4 teaspoon
Hi-Altar Incense	1/2 teaspoon
Blessing Incense	1 teaspoon
Holiness Trinity Incense	1/4 teaspoon
Spiritual Inspiration Incense	1/2 teaspoon

When the above is thoroughly mixed, sprinkle the table or altar with a small amount of **Holy Prophet Powder**. Then put the incense blend in your two incense burners on the table or altar and light. Sprinkle a small amount of **Gospel Oil, Myrtle Oil, and Jerusalem Oil** on your naked body. Now close your eyes and concentrate on your illness or that of a friend for a full seven minutes. When finished, rise and blow out the candles. Repeat this entire ritual for seven consecutive days at the exact same time.

Special Spell to Help Avoid Accidents

Arrange the table or altar as illustrated in Chapter two. Light your two Monthly Vibratory Candles and your two Daily Cross Candles. Then carefully blend the following ingredients in a plain white dish:

King Solomon Incense	1/4 teaspoon
Faith, Hope and Charity Incense	1/4 teaspoon
Lord's Ressurection Incense	1/2 teaspoon
Blessing of Allah Incense	1 teaspoon
Bible Bouquet Incense	1/4 teaspoon
Exodus Incense	1/4 teaspoon

When the above is thoroughly mixed, sprinkle the table or altar with a small amount of **Devil's Shoestring Oil, Psalm Oil, and Sandalwood Oil.** Then put the incense blend in your two incense burners on the table or altar and light. Sprinkle a small amount of **Jehovah Vision Powder, Wormwood Powder, and Mount Zion Powder** on your naked body. Now close your eyes and concentrate on avoiding accidents for a full seven minutes. When finished, rise and blow out the candles. Repeat this entire ritual for seven successive days at the exact same time.

To Escape All Forms of Serious Sickness

Arrange the table or altar as illustrated in Chapter two. Light your two Monthly Vibratory Candles and your two Daily Cross Candles. Then carefully blend the following ingredients in a plain white dish:

Peace Incense	1 teaspoon
Sandalwood Incense	1/2 teaspoon
Holiness of the Lord Incense	1 teaspoon
Beneficial Incense	1/4 teaspoon
Kindly Spirit Incense	1/4 teaspoon

When thoroughly mixed, sprinkle the table or altar with a small amount of **Deliverance Powder and Special Benediction Powder.** Then put the incense blend in your two incense burners on the table or altar and light. Sprinkle a small amount of *World's Wonder Oil and Balm of Gilead Oil* on your naked body. Now close your eyes and concentrate on avoiding all sickness for a full seven minutes. When finished, rise and bloats out the candles. Repeat this entire ritual for seven successive days at the exact same time.

TO MAKE A SICK PERSON FEEL MUCH BETTER

Arrange the table or altar as illustrated in Chapter two. Light your two Monthly Vibratory Candles and your two Daily Cross Candles. Then carefully blend the following ingredients in a plain white dish:

Coconut Incense	1 teaspoon
Tobacco Incense	1/4 teaspoon
Blessing of Allah Incense	1/4 teaspoon
Healing Incense	1/2 teaspoon
Ten Commandments Incense	1 teaspoon

When the above is thoroughly blended, put the mixture in your two incense burners on the table or altar and light. Then close your eyes and concentrate on the spell's purpose for a full seven minutes. Lastly, repeat the following benediction three times:

"Good tidings, dear holy day! Take away the bad feelings from (name of person or yourself), take away the fevers. O thou dear Lord Jesus Christ, take this illness away from him (her) this moment."

This spell must always be cast on a Thursday for the first time, on Friday for the second time, and on Saturday for the third time. The benediction must be repeated three times each day, and then not a word dare be spoken to anyone until the sun has risen. Neither dare the sick person speak to anyone until after sunrise. The person working the spell must not eat pork, nor drink milk, nor cross running water, for a period of nine days after. When finished, rise and blow out the candles. Then have the sick person in perfect soberness and without having spoken to anyone, catch some rain in a pot, before sunrise. He or she must boil an egg in this water and when cooled, bore three holes in this egg with a new needle. The egg is then to be carried to an active ant hill and left. The sick person will feel relieved as soon as the egg has been eaten. This spell, an old gypsy concoction, is said to never fail when undertaken by true believers.

To Stop Mental Illness

Arrange the table or altar as illustrated in Chapter two. Light your two Monthly Vibratory Candles and your two Daily Cross Candles. Then carefully blend the following ingredients in a plain white dish:

Spiritualist Incense	1 teaspoon
Conquering Incense	1 teaspoon
Invocation Incense	1/2 teaspoon
Mohammed Temple Incense	1/2 teaspoon

When the above is thoroughly mixed, sprinkle the table or altar with a small amount of **Freedom Oil, All Saints Oil, and Hi-Altar Oil.** Then put the incense blend in your two incense burners on the table or altar and light. Sprinkle a small amount of **Mount Sinai Powder and Hand of Glory Powder** on your naked body. Now close your eyes and concentrate on the mental problem for a full seven minutes. When finished, rise and blow out the candles. Repeat this entire ritual for seven successive days at the exact same time.

SECRET SPELLS AGAINST ILLNESS & DEATH

TO PREVENT ANY PHYSICAL HARM

Arrange the table or altar as illustrated in Chapter two. Light your two Monthly Vibratory Candles and your two Daily Cross Candles. Then carefully blend the following ingredients in a plain white dish:

10 Commandments Incense	*1 teaspoon*
King Midas Incense	*1/4 teaspoon*
Merciful Heaven Incense	*1/2 teaspoon*
Spiritual Vision Incense	*1 teaspoon*
7 Holy Herbs Incense	*1/2 teaspoon*
All Saints Incense	*1/2 teaspoon*

When the above is thoroughly mixed, sprinkle the table or altar with a small amount of **Garden of Eden Oil and King Solomon Oil.** Then put the incense blend in your two incense burners on the table or altar and light. Sprinkle a small amount of **Blessing Powder and Hallelujah Powder** on your naked body. Now close your eyes and concentrate on avoiding any untimely physical harm for a full seven minutes. When finished, rise and blow out the candles. Repeat this entire ritual for seven successive days at the exact same time.

SPECIAL SPELL TO PROTECT AGAINST UNTIMELY DEATH

Arrange the table or altar as illustrated in Chapter two. Light your two Monthly Vibratory Candles and your two Daily Cross Candles. Then carefully blend the following ingredients in a plain white dish:

Protection Incense	*1 teaspoon*
Ground Devils Shoestring	*1/4 teaspoon*
Rose of Crucifixion Incense	*1/4 teaspoon*
Holy Sanctuary Incense	*1/4 teaspoon*
Power Incense	*1/2 teaspoon*

When the above is thoroughly mixed, sprinkle the table or altar with a small amount of **Messiah's Message Powder and Holy Rites of the Lord Powder.** Then put the incense blend in your two incense burners on the table or altar and light. Sprinkle a small amount of **Moses Oil, Lotus Blossom Oil, and Beneficial Oil** on your naked body. Now close your eyes and concentrate on death for a full seven minutes. When finished, rise and blow out the candles. Repeat this entire ritual for seven successive days at the exact same time.

To Relieve Pain During Illness

Arrange the table or altar as illustrated in Chapter two. Light your two Monthly Vibratory Candles and your two Daily Cross Candles. Then carefully blend the following ingredients in a plain white dish:

Merciful Heaven Incense	1/2 teaspoon
Spiritual Inspiration Incense	1 teaspoon
Deliverance Incense	1 teaspoon
Mecca Incense	1/4 teaspoon

When the above is thoroughly blended, put the mixture in your two incense burners on the table or altar and light. Then close your eyes and concentrate on the spell's purpose for a full seven minutes. Lastly, repeat the following benediction three times:

"Jesus Christ, dearest blood! That stoppeth the pain and stoppeth the blood. In this please help (name of person in pain, or your own name if you have the pain). O God the Father, God the Son, God the Holy Ghost. Amen, Amen. Amen."

When finished, rise and blow out the candles. Then run your thumbs along the sick person's body, or your own if you are the one in pain. Start just under the ribs and go all the way down to the thighs. Speak not another word for the spell is now cast.

14

SECRET SPELLS FOR THE DESTRUCTION OF EVIL

TO FORCE AN ENEMY TO STOP HARMING YOU

Arrange the table or altar as illustrated in Chapter 2. Light your two Monthly Vibratory Candles and your two Daily Cross Candles. Then carefully blend the following ingredients in a plain white dish:

Compelling Incense	1 teaspoon
Uncrossing Incense	1/2 teaspoon
Confusion Incense	1/2 teaspoon
Compelling Incense	1/2 teaspoon
Hair of enemy	3 strands

When the above is thoroughly mixed, sprinkle the table or altar with a small amount of **Black Art Oil** and **Uncrossing Oil**. Then put the incense blend in your two incense burners on the table or altar and light. Sprinkle a small amount of **Uncrossing Powder** on your naked body. Now close your eyes and concentrate on your enemy for a full seven minutes. When finished, rise and blow out the candles. Repeat this entire ritual for seven successive days at the exact same time.

To Break the Influence of an Evil Spell

Arrange the table or altar as illustrated in Chapter 2. Light your two Monthly Vibratory Candles and your two Daily Cross Candles. Then carefully blend the following ingredients in a plain white dish:

Graveyard Dust	1/4 teaspoon
Hair of Enemy	7 strands
Black Cat Incense	1 teaspoon
Commanding Incense	1 teaspoon
Lucky Rites Incense	1/4 teaspoon
Tansy Powder	1/4 teaspoon

When the above is thoroughly mixed, sprinkle the table or altar with a small amount of *Protection Powder* and *Invocation Powder*. Then put the incense blend in your two incense burners on the table or altar and light. Anoint your body with a small amount of *Indian Guide Oil* and *Jinx Removing Oil*. Now close your eyes and concentrate on your enemy for a full seven minutes. When finished, rise and blow out the candles. Repeat this entire ritual for seven successive days at the exact same time.

To Eliminate Danger From Your Life

Arrange the table or altar as illustrated in Chapter two. Light your two Monthly Vibratory Candles and your two Daily Cross Candles. Then carefully blend the following ingredients in a plain white dish:

Sandlewood Incense	1/4 teaspoon
Frankincense	1/2 teaspoon
John the Conqueror Incense	1/2 teaspoon
Myrrh Incense	1/4 teaspoon
Sage Powder	1/4 teaspoon
Jinx Removing Incense	1/2 teaspoon

When the above is thoroughly mixed, sprinkle the table or altar with a small amount of *Spikenard Powder and Black Cat Bone Powder*. Then put the incense blend in your two incense

SECRET SPELLS FOR THE DESTRUCTION OF EVIL

burners on the table or altar and light. Anoint your body with a small amount of ***Special Perfume Oil No. 20*** and ***Bend Over Oil.*** Close your eyes and concentrate on the problem for a full seven minutes. When finished, rise and blow out the candles. Repeat entire ritual for 7 successive days at the exact same time.

TO STOP THE EFFECTS OF AN EVIL EYE SPELL

Arrange the table or altar as illustrated in Chapter 2. Light your two Monthly Vibratory Candles and your two Daily Cross Candles. Then carefully blend the following ingredients in a plain white dish:

Frankincense Powder	*1/4 teaspoon*
XX Double Cross Incense	*1 teaspoon*
Satan Begone Incense	*1 teaspoon*
Genuine Brahma Incense	*1/4 teaspoon*
7 Holy Spirits Incense	*1/4 teaspoon*
Rosemary Oil Incense	*1/4 teaspoon*

When the above is thoroughly mixed, sprinkle the table or altar with a small amount of ***Concentration Oil, Rose Oil,*** and ***Magnet Oil.*** Then put the incense blend in your two incense burners on the table or altar and light. Anoint your body with a small amount of ***Sage Powder*** and ***Crossing Powder.*** Now close your eyes and concentrate on the problem for a full seven minutes. When finished, rise and blow out the candles. Repeat this entire ritual for seven successive days at the exact same time.

TO FORCE A MALICIOUS PERSON TO LEAVE YOU ALONE

Arrange the table or altar as illustrated in Chapter two. Light your two Monthly Vibratory Candles and your two Daily Cross Candles. Then carefully blend the following ingredients in a plain white dish:

Go Away Evil Incense	*1/2 teaspoon*
Conquering Glory Incense	*1 teaspoon*
Crown of Success Incense	*1/2 teaspoon*

When the above is thoroughly blended, put the mixture in your two incense burners on the table or altar and light. Then close your eyes and concentrate on the spell's purpose for a full seven minutes. Lastly, repeat the following benediction three times:

*"Dullix, ix, ux. Yea, you cannot come over Pontio.
Pontio is highly above Pilato."*

When finished, rise and blow out the candles. Repeat this entire ritual for seven successive days at the exact same time. Then, just before going to bed that night, say this benediction:

*"Three holy men went out walking,
They did bless this troubled person;
They blessed that trouble might not increase,
They blessed that trouble might quickly cease!"*

A Powerful Evil Destroying Charm

Arrange the table or altar as illustrated in Chapter two. Light your two Monthly Vibratory Candles and your two Daily Cross Candles. Then carefully blend the following ingredients in a plain white dish:

Crossing Incense	1 teaspoon
Dragon Blood Incense	1/2 teaspoon
Power Incense	1 teaspoon
Fingernail parings of enemy	7 pieces
Ground Patchouly Leaves	1/2 teaspoon

When the above is thoroughly mixed, sprinkle the table or altar with a small amount of **Bat's Blood Oil** and **Jinx Removing Oil**. Then put the incense blend in your two incense burners on the table or altar and light. Sprinkle a small amount of **Jinx Removing Powder** and **Fast Luck Powder** on your naked body. Now close your eyes and concentrate on the evil for a full seven minutes. When finished, rise and blow out the candles. Repeat this entire ritual for seven successive days at the exact same time.

SECRET SPELLS FOR THE DESTRUCTION OF EVIL

TO REVERSE A BAD SPELL'S DISASTROUS EFFECT

Arrange the table or altar as illustrated in Chapter two. Light your two Monthly Vibratory Candles and your two Daily Cross Candles. Then carefully blend the following ingredients in a plain white dish:

Van Van Incense	*1 teaspoon*
Black Cat Incense	*1/4 teaspoon*
Lodestone Incense	*1/4 teaspoon*
Confusion Powder	*1/2 teaspoon*
Protection Powder	*1/2 teaspoon*

When the above is thoroughly mixed, sprinkle the table or altar with a small amount of **Devil's Shoestring Powder** and **Ground Smellage Root**. Then put the incense blend in your two incense burners on the table or altar and light. Sprinkle a small amount of **Dove's Blood Oil** and **High Conquering Oil** on your naked body. Now close your eyes and concentrate on the evil spell you are trying to break. Do this for a full seven minutes. When finished, rise and blow out the candles. Repeat this entire ritual for seven successive days at the exact same time.

TO MAKE SOMEONE STOP HEXING YOU

Arrange the table or altar as illustrated in Chapter two. Light your two Monthly Vibratory Candles and your two Daily Cross Candles. Then carefully blend the following ingredients in a plain white dish:

Controlling Incense	*1/2 teaspoon*
Crushed Cinnamon	*1/4 teaspoon*
Peace Incense	*1/4 teaspoon*
Red Storax Incense	*1/2 teaspoon*
Yohimbehe Bark Incense	*1/4 teaspoon*
Bamba Wood Incense	*1/4 teaspoon*

When the above is thoroughly mixed, sprinkle the table or altar with a small amount of **Lavendar Powder, Orris Powder,** and **Patchouly Powder**. Then put the incense blend in your two incense burners on the table or altar and light. Sprinkle a small amount of **Bat's Heart Oil** and **Cassia Oil** on your naked body. Now close your eyes and concentrate on your enemy for a full seven minutes. When finished, rise and blow out the candles. Repeat this entire ritual for seven consecutive days at the exact same time.

To Defeat a Dangerous Rival

Arrange the table or altar as illustrated in Chapter two. Light your two Monthly Vibratory Candles and your two Daily Cross Candles. Then carefully blend the following ingredients in a plain white dish:

Ground Archangel Herb	1/4 teaspoon
Vishnu Incense	1/2 teaspoon
Bible Incense	1/4 teaspoon
Dragon Blood Incense	1/4 teaspoon
Lucky Planet Incense	1/4 teaspoon
Justo Juez Incense	1/2 teaspoon

When the above is thoroughly mixed, sprinkle the table or altar with a small amount of **Cleopatra Oil** and **High Conquering Oil**. Then put the incense blend in your two incense burners on the table or altar and light. Sprinkle a small amount of **Lodestone Powder, Vision Powder,** and **Invocation Powder** on your naked body. Now close your eyes and concentrate on your rival for a full seven minutes. When finished, rise and blow out the candles. Repeat this entire ritual for seven successive days at the exact same time.

To Bind a Person Who is Exerting Evil Power

Arrange the table or altar as illustrated in Chapter two. Light your two Monthly Vibratory Candles and your two Daily Cross Candles. Then carefully blend the following ingredients in a plain white dish:

Conquering Glory Incense	*1/2 teaspoon*
Kindly Spirits Incense	*1/2 teaspoon*
Success Incense	*1/4 teaspoon*
Separation Incense	*1/4 teaspoon*
Healing Incense	*1/2 teaspoon*

When the above is thoroughly blended, put the mixture in your two incense burners on the table or altar and light. Then close your eyes and concentrate on the evil person for a full seven minutes. Lastly, repeat the following benediction three times:

"O Peter, O Peter, borrow the power from God; what I shall bind with the bands of a Christian hand, shall stay bound, shall be bound. All male and female sinners, be they great or small, young or old, shall be spell bound by the power of God, and not be able to walk forward or backward until I see them with my eyes, and give them leave with my tongue, except it be that they count for me all the stones that may be between heaven and earth, all rain drops, all the leaves and all the grasses in the world. This I pray for the repentance of my enemies."

When finished, rise and blow out the candles. Early the next morning, before sunrise, take three nails and go stand under a young tree. Hold these nails toward the rising sun and again repeat the above benediction. Return to your home, wrap the nails in clean black cotton cloth. and hide them in the corner of a dark closet. No one must he able to accidentally come across these sacred nails. Then recite the Lord's Prayer three times.

Helping Yourself with Magickal Oils A-Z

Maria Solomon

There are over *1000 Oils*
included in this *A-Z Guide*
written to help anyone use the
vast magickal powers of oils to achieve their goals.

This book is packed with
charms, spells, rituals and formulas
all of which can be used by any person
who has sufficient belief and desire to do so.
Let the mystical powers of oils bring
prosperity and balance to all aspects of your life,
health, wealth, love and more!!

$7.95

Love
Charms & Spells
by Jade
$5.95

Over 100 Spells, Rituals and Potions for Love,
all of which can be used by any sincere person
who has sufficient belief and desire
to do so.

Chapters in this book include:

Get the One You Want
Love Potions and Other Recipes
Solving Love Problems
Keeping Your Lover
Unwanted Love

VOODOO
CHARMS & TALISMANS

Robert Pelton

The power of Voodoo can be yours today!
Absolutely authentic and easy-to-follow instructions to:

- Make your own talismans
- Concoct your own love potions
- Win at games of chance
- Summon spirits
- Defend yourself against those who may wish you ill
- Attack your enemies through devastating spells

Here are the words, the symbols and the ingredients. Here is all you need to know to possess power beyond your imagination!

$8.95

Draja Mickaharic
A Century of Spells

A collection of over one hundred useful spells . . . that work!
By the author of the best-selling *Spiritual Cleansing*

A Century of Spells

Draja Mickaharic

This book is a practical introduction to natural magic. It is a workbook designed to help you learn magic and it can serve as a practical reference for any practicing magician. You will learn to work with a number of many different spells from many different magical traditions. Here you'll find clear, complete instructions for making and working with water spells, baths, powders, incense, oils and herbs. Learn how to:
- protect yourself against negativity
- reverse spells that have been directed at you
- use spells for healing, good fortune, drawing companionship, protecting your home, cleaning your aura, growing spiritually and more!

$8.95

ORIGINAL PUBLICATIONS

Our catalog of over 500 titles published or distributed by Original Publications includes books on Santeria, Yoruba, Voodoo, Candle Burning, Herbs Oils, Spiritualism, Spells, Numerology, Dreams, Kabbalah, Wicca, Magic, Occult Science, Natural Medicine, Nutrition, Healing, Self Help, Prayer, Astrology, Divination, Tarot, and Spanish Language. For a complete catalog **CHECK THIS BOX** and send $2.00 to the address listed below. ☐

*VIEW OUR CATALOG AND PLACE YOUR ORDERS ON OUR **SECURED WEBSITE***
WWW.ORIGINALPUBLICATIONS.COM

☐ **HELPING YOURSELF WITH SELECTED PRAYERS** $4.95
☐ **SPIRITUAL CLEANSING: A Handbook of Psychic Protection;** Mickaharic $6.95
☐ **MYSTERY OF LONG LOST 8,9,10 BOOKS OF MOSES;** Gamache $4.95
☐ **NEW REV. 6&7 BKS. OF MOSES & MGC USES OF PSALMS** Wippler $8.95
☐ **MASTER BOOK OF CANDLE BURNING;** Gamache $4.95
☐ **HELPING YOURSELF WITH MAGICKAL OILS A-Z** Maria Solomon $7.95
☐ **VOODOO CHARMS & TALISMANS;** Robert Pelton $8.95
☐ **MONEY SPELLS & CHARMS** by Jade - $4.95
☐ **LOVE SPELLS & CHARMS** by Jade - $5.95
☐ **PROTECTION CHARMS & SPELLS** by Jade-$5.95
☐ **SANTERIA: African Magic in Latin America;** Wippler $10.95
☐ **RITUALS & SPELLS OF SANTERIA;** Wippler $7.95
☐ **OLODUMARE; God in Yoruba Belief,** Idowu $14.95
☐ **HERBAL BATHS OF SANTERIA;** Montenegro $5.95
☐ **POWERFUL AMULETS OF SANTERIA;** Montenegro $9.95
☐ **POWERS OF THE ORISHAS;** Wippler $8.95
☐ **TALES OF YORUBA GODS & HEROES;** Courlander $11.95
☐ **A CENTURY OF SPELLS** - Mickaharic - $8.95
☐ **IBA SE ORISA; Ifa Proverbs,History & Prayer** - $14.95
☐ **THE MAGIC CANDLE;** Dey - $4.95
☐ **ESU- ELEGBA Ifa and the Divine Messenger;** Fatunmbi $4.95
☐ **OGUN: Ifa & the Spirit of Iron;** Fatunmbi $4.95
☐ **OCHOSI: Ifa & the Spirit of the Tracker;** Fatunmbi $4.95
☐ **OBATALA: Ifa & the Spirit of the White Cloth;** Fatunmbi $4.95
☐ **SHANGO: Ifa & the Spirit of Lightning;** Fatunmbi $4.95
☐ **OSHUN: Ifa & the Spirit of the River;** Fatunmbi $4.95
☐ **YEMOJA/OLOKUN: Ifa & the Spirit of the Ocean;** Fatunmbi $4.95
☐ **OYA: Ifa & the Spirit of the Wind;** Fatunmbi $4.95

NAME _____ TELEPHONE _____

ADDRESS _____

CITY _____ STATE _____ ZIP _____

*TO ORDER BY MASTERCARD, VISA OR AMERICAN EXPRESS
CALL TOLL FREE (888) 622-8581 -OR- (516) 454-6809.*

TO ORDER BY MAIL: CHECK THE BOXES NEXT TO YOUR SELECTIONS. ADD THE TOTAL. SHIPPING COSTS ARE $3.00 FOR THE FIRST BOOK PLUS 50 CENTS FOR EACH ADDITIONAL BOOK. NEW YORK STATE RESIDENTS PLEASE ADD 8.25% SALES TAX. ALL ORDERS SHIP IN 14 DAYS. SORRY, NO C.O.D.'S. **SEND ORDERS TO THE ADDRESS BELOW.**

ORIGINAL PUBLICATIONS • P.O. BOX 236, OLD BETHPAGE, NY 11804-0236

WHITE MAGIC